T0001643

NATIONAL GEOGRAPHIC KiDS
LITTLE KIDS
FIRST
BIG
BOOK OF
WHY
2

CHAMPION TAEKWONDO

LITTLE KIDS FIRST BIG BOOK OF WHY 2

Jill Esbaum

NATIONAL GEOGRAPHIC KiDS
WASHINGTON, D.C.

CONTENTS

ME, MYSELF, AND I 6
Why Are People's Voices Different? 8
Why Can't I Run as Fast as a Dog? 10
Why Does My Heart Beat Fast When I Exercise? 12
Try This! Test Your Ticker 13
Why Do I Blush? 14
Why Does a Bruise Turn Colors? 15
Why Do I Shiver When I'm Cold? 16
Why Do My Feet Stink Sometimes? 18
Why Am I Ticklish? 20
Try This! Tickle Your Tootsies 21
Why Do I Yawn? 22
Why Do I Have Eyelashes? 24
Why Do I Have Eyebrows? 25
Why Do I Cry? 26
Why Does My Stomach Growl When I'm Hungry? 28
Why Do I Burp? 30
Why Do I Sneeze? 32
Let's Play a Game! 34

FUN AND GAMES 36
Why Does Music Make Me Move? 38
Why Are Bubbles Always Round? 40
Why Do Kites Have Tails? 42
Why Are Swimming Pools Blue? 44
Why Do Some Swimmers Wear Goggles? 45
Why Do Martial Arts Have Colored Belts? 46
Why Do Balls Bounce? 48
Try This! Bouncy, Bouncy 49
Why Do Referees "Talk" With Their Hands? 50
Why Can't We Feed Animals at the Zoo? 52
Why Do Roller Coasters Make Me Feel Funny? 54
Why Does Spinning Make Me Dizzy? 55
Why Does Cotton Candy Melt in My Mouth? 56
Try This! Dissolving Sugar 57
Why Are Fireworks So Loud? 58
Let's Play a Game! 60

AWESOME ANIMALS 62
Why Do Dogs Sniff Everything? 64
Try This! Test Your Sniffer 65
Why Do a Cat's Eyes Shine at Night? 66
Why Do Some Animals Live Underground? 68
Why Do Monkeys Live in Trees? 70
Why Are Some Animals So Colorful? 72
Why Do Kangaroos Have Pouches? 74
Why Do Moose Have Antlers? 76
Why Do Bats Fly at Night? 78
Try This! Find That Moth! 79
Why Do Fireflies Glow? 80
Why Do Skunks Stink? 82
Why Don't Penguins Get Cold? 84
Why Do Walruses Have Such Long Tusks? 86
Why Do Wolves Live in Packs? 88
Why Do Birds Sing? 90
Try This! Time for a Song 91
Why Are Dinosaur Names So Long? 92
Let's Play a Game! 94

NATURE ALL AROUND 96
Why Is Ocean Water So Salty? 98
Why Does Fog Feel Wet? 100
Why Is Grass Wet in the Morning? 101
Why Do Puddles Disappear? 102
Try This! Where'd the Water Go? 103
Why Does Sunshine Feel Hot? 104
Why Does My Shadow Change Shape? 106
Try This! Shifting Shadows 107
Why Do Pumpkins Have So Many Seeds? 108
Why Are There So Many Kinds of Flowers? 110
Why Do Weeds Grow in Gardens? 112
Why Do Mushrooms Grow on Some Trees? 114
Why Don't Trees Fall Over? 116
Why Are Some Deserts So Hot and Dry? 118
Why Does the Sun Rise and Set? 120
Try This! Day Into Night Into Day 121
Let's Play a Game! 122

Parent Tips 124
Glossary 125
Additional Resources 126
Index 126
Credits and Acknowledgments 128

CHAPTER 1

ME, MYSELF, AND I

You sneeze, ah-CHOO! Your stomach growls, grumble-rumble. Your heart races, lub-dub-lub-dub-lub-dub. Your body is amazing, and there's a reason for everything it does.

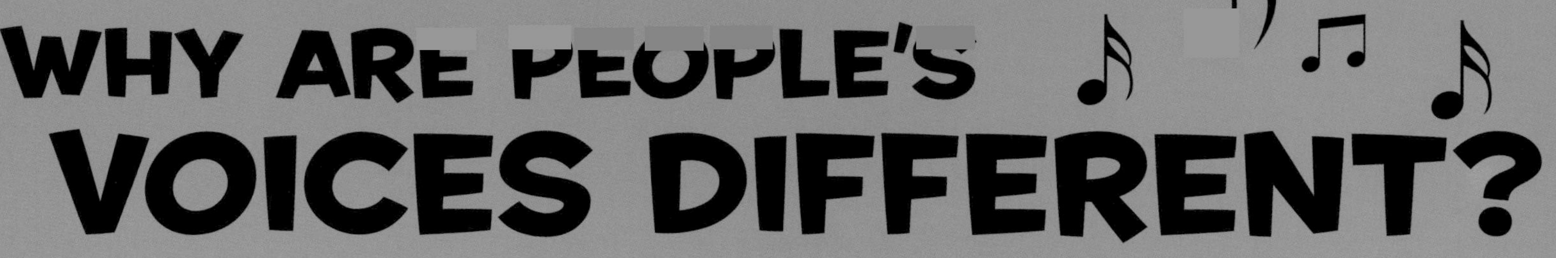

WHY ARE PEOPLE'S VOICES DIFFERENT?

Your one-of-a-kind voice is a remarkable instrument. Your words help you communicate, of course, but even the sound of your voice lets people know if you're feeling happy or sad, excited or angry, worried or afraid, and so much more. Because no two people's vocal cords and mouths are exactly the same, each has a voice unlike anybody else's.

SINGING works the same way as **SPEAKING.** Each of us has a singing **VOICE** unlike anybody else's. **LA-LA-LA!**

The **FASTER** a person's **VOCAL CORDS VIBRATE,** the **HIGHER** their **VOICE** will sound.

Your voice starts with a huff of air coming up from your lungs. The air moves across your voice box, called the larynx (say LARE-ingks). In your larynx are folds of thin skin called vocal cords. When air passes across the cords, it causes them to move back and forth, or vibrate. This makes sound, which goes into your mouth.

Your mouth's size and shape, as well as your tongue, your lips and cheeks, and even your teeth, work together to create a voice that your family and friends instantly recognize as YOU.

WHY CAN'T I RUN AS FAST AS A DOG?

A dog's bones and muscles are made to move more quickly than ours. Scientists say our bodies might be able to move at speeds of up to 40 miles an hour (64 km/h)—but nobody has come close to that yet.

If you want to win a foot race against an animal, challenge a chicken. Its top speed is only about nine miles an hour (14 km/h).

Have you ever run in a race?

The **WORLD'S FASTEST DOG** is the **GREYHOUND.** It can **RUN 43 MILES AN HOUR** (69 km/h).

The **WORLD'S FASTEST HUMAN** is currently **USAIN BOLT.** He **RAN** more than **27 MILES AN HOUR** (43 km/h) for a short **DISTANCE.**

WHY DOES MY HEART BEAT FAST WHEN I EXERCISE?

Like other **MUSCLES, HEARTS** get **STRONGER** with regular **EXERCISE.**

FACTS

Your heart is the size of your fist.

Your rib cage protects your heart.

Of all the muscles in your body, your heart works the hardest.

Your heart beats about 100,000 times a day.

Your heart is a muscle that pumps blood through your body. That blood has important jobs to do. It carries oxygen to every part of you, along with everything else your body needs to stay healthy. It also carries away waste.

When you exercise, your body works harder. It needs more oxygen—fast! Your heart speeds up, pumping harder to keep blood flowing to where it's needed.

TRY THIS! TEST YOUR TICKER

YOU'LL NEED

a stopwatch or a watch with a second hand

paper and a pen or pencil

1 Sit down, then push your fingertips against the front of your neck, just to the side of your windpipe.

2 Count how many beats you feel in one minute. Write down that number.

3 Do 20 jumping jacks, then count the beats again for one minute. Write down that number.

4 Did your heart beat faster or slower after exercising? Rest one minute, then count again. Has it slowed down?

WHY DO I BLUSH?

Nobody knows why blushing happens. But embarrassing moments happen to all humans. That "everybody's looking at me" feeling can make your cheeks feel hot. You know they're getting red, red, RED.

What kinds of things make you feel embarrassed?

That redness is because of tiny veins just under your skin. For some reason, when you feel embarrassed, your brain tells those veins to open wider. Blood floods into them, and your skin looks red.

BLOOD VESSELS are TUBES that carry blood throughout your BODY. Some are as BIG around as an ADULT'S THUMB. Others are SMALLER than one of your HAIRS.

WHY DOES A BRUISE TURN COLORS?

Imagine you bump your knee—ow, that hurt! There's no cut, but small blood vessels under your skin were damaged. A little blood leaked out of them. That shows through your skin as a red area.

But don't worry. Your body is already working to heal itself, to break up and reabsorb that blood. Soon that red bruise turns bluish-purple. Over the next few days, it turns greenish-yellow, then light brown. In a week or two, you'll check the bruise and—hey, where'd it go?

SCIENTISTS say that TELLING somebody they're BLUSHING—even when they are not—can make them BLUSH.

WHY DO I SHIVER WHEN I'M COLD?

One of your brain's jobs is to keep your body temperature at about 98.6°F (37°C). When your skin gets too cool, it shoots signals to your brain, which begins a warming trick. It makes your muscles tense up, relax, tense up, relax—super fast. That's shivering!

Can you guess what all that shivering does? It creates heat!

What makes you shiver?

HOW DO I GET GOOSEBUMPS?

Your skin is covered with tiny hairs. When you shiver, your muscles tighten, and those hairs stand up. At the bottom of each hair, a bump rises, too.

SKIN WITH GOOSEBUMPS

You can also get goosebumps when you are hit with strong feelings such as surprise or fear.

Have you ever seen how the **FUR** on a **CAT'S BACK** stands **UP** when it's **AFRAID?** At the **BOTTOM** of those **HAIRS,** that cat's skin is **GOOSEBUMPY, TOO!**

WHY DO MY FEET STINK SOMETIMES?

Tiny creatures called bacteria are living on your feet. Don't bother looking, because you cannot see them without a microscope. What are the bacteria doing down there? Eating dead skin cells and oils that come out of your skin.

BACTERIA
(say back-TEER-ee-uh)
are EVERYWHERE,
on and inside every
LIVING THING.

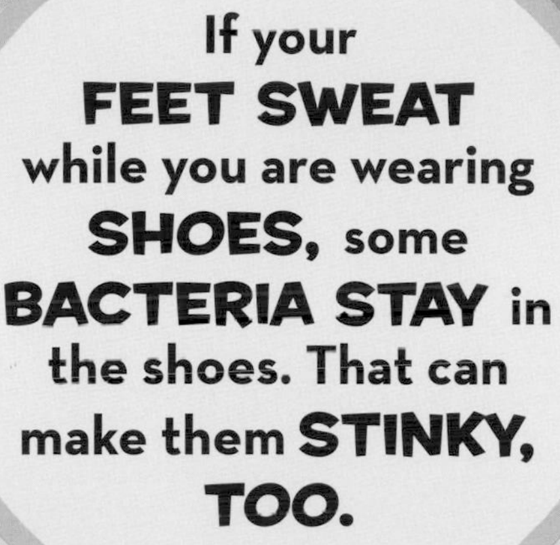

If your **FEET SWEAT** while you are wearing **SHOES,** some **BACTERIA STAY** in the shoes. That can make them **STINKY, TOO.**

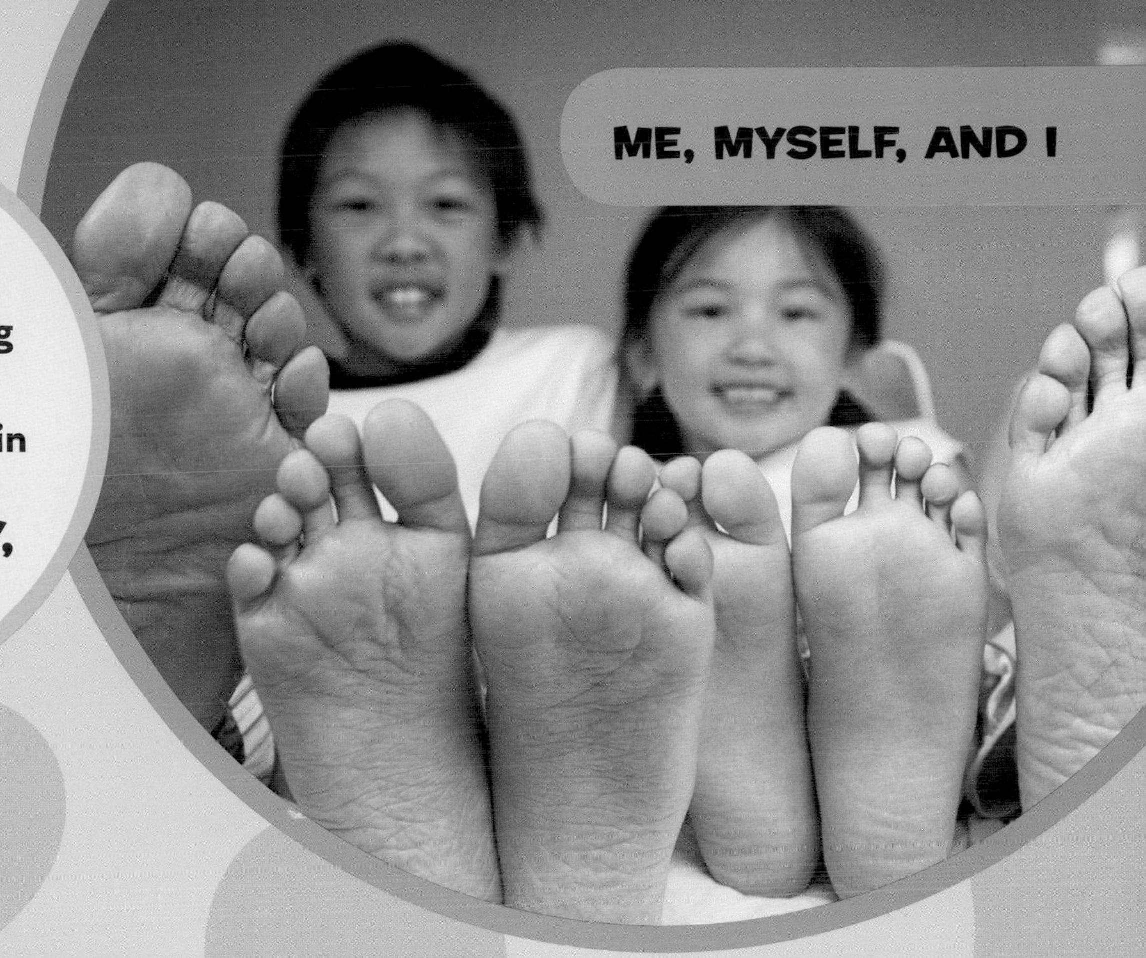

When your feet get hot and sweaty, more bacteria grow. To get rid of their waste, they put out an acid. That acid STINKS.

So the next time someone tells you your feet stink, you can tell them it isn't really your feet that smell. It's the bacteria living on them.

WHY AM I TICKLISH?

Nobody knows for sure exactly why humans are ticklish. But most of us have places more sensitive than others to a tickly touch—our armpits, our ribs, and especially our feet. Scientists say it's nearly impossible to tickle ourselves. Why? Because our brains are too smart. They already know exactly where those fingers of ours are headed.

Many apes and monkeys giggle when tickled. Scientists have even tickled rats. Large animals like giraffes and elephants shiver when an insect lands on their skin. That's a sort of ticklish reaction, too.

TRY THIS! TICKLE YOUR TOOTSIES

Can you tickle yourself? Give it a try.

1 Sit down and softly wiggle your fingers over the bottom of your bare foot. Does it feel ticklish?

2 Now close your eyes and have someone you trust softly tickle the bottom of your foot. Does that feel more or less ticklish than doing it yourself?

WHY DO I YAWN?

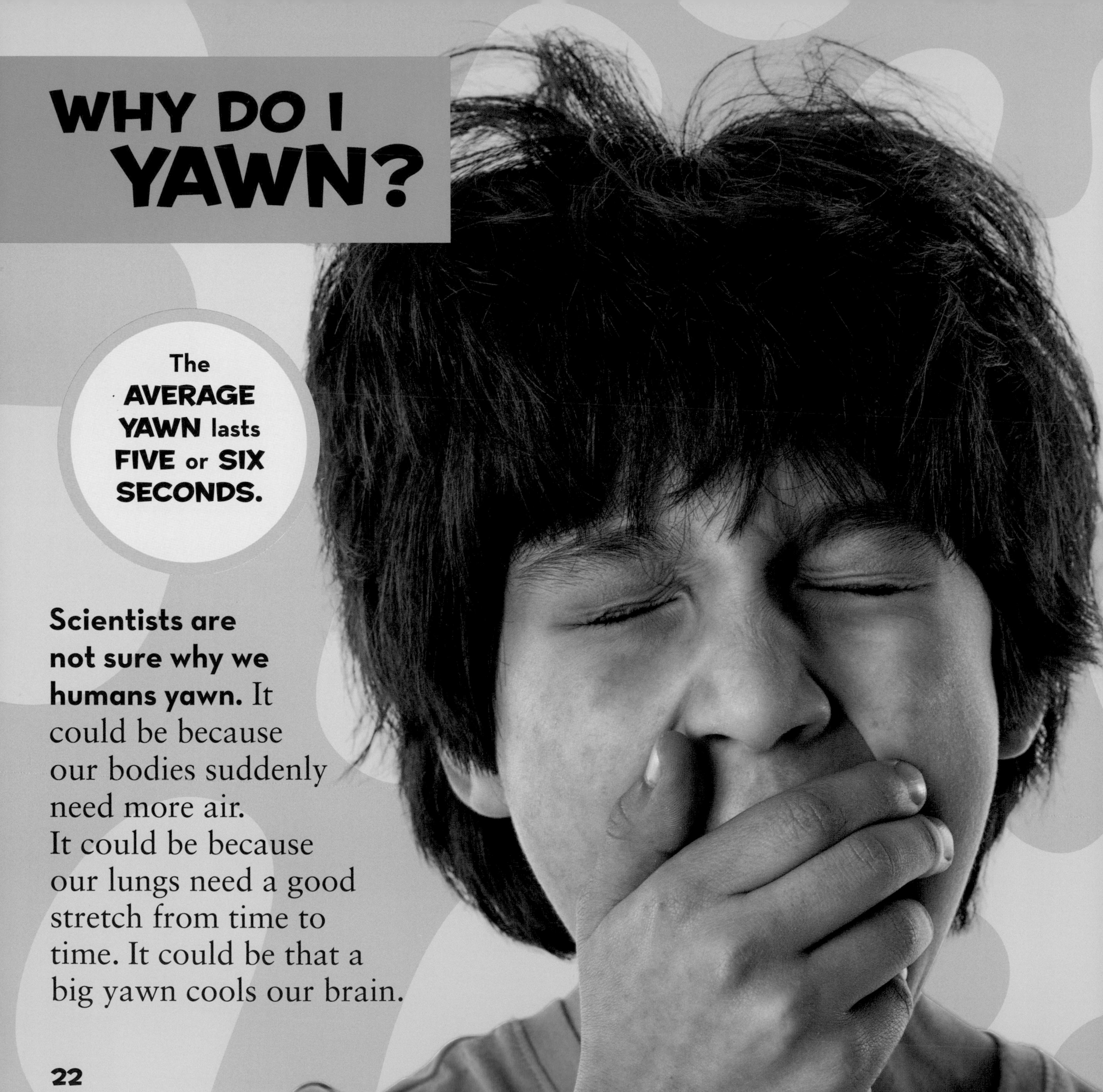

The **AVERAGE YAWN** lasts **FIVE** or **SIX SECONDS.**

Scientists are not sure why we humans yawn. It could be because our bodies suddenly need more air. It could be because our lungs need a good stretch from time to time. It could be that a big yawn cools our brain.

ANIMALS YAWN, TOO— probably for the same reasons **HUMANS** do.

Did reading this page and seeing these pictures make you yawn?

What we do know is that yawns often happen when we're tired or bored. We also know that seeing someone else yawn can actually make us yawn—whether we want to or not. Our bodies simply take over, and—whoops—here comes another one!

Even **READING** about somebody **YAWNING** can make you **YAWN.**

WHY DO I HAVE EYELASHES?

Some **ANIMALS** have **REALLY LONG LASHES.** Check out the lashes on this giraffe.

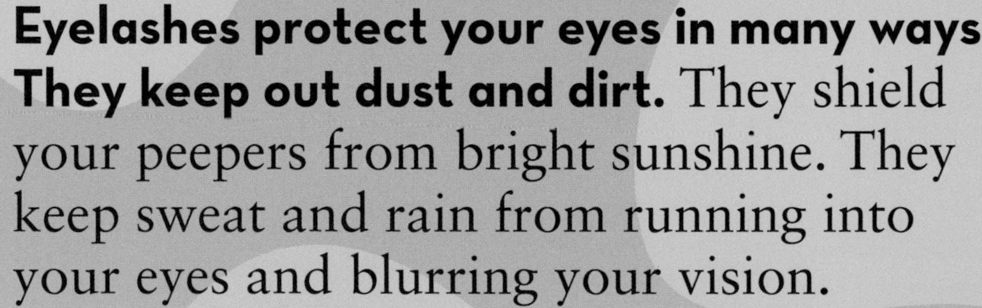

Eyelashes protect your eyes in many ways. They keep out dust and dirt. They shield your peepers from bright sunshine. They keep sweat and rain from running into your eyes and blurring your vision.

When you lose an eyelash, it grows back. Whew. That's good, because you need those lashes!

WHY DO I HAVE EYEBROWS?

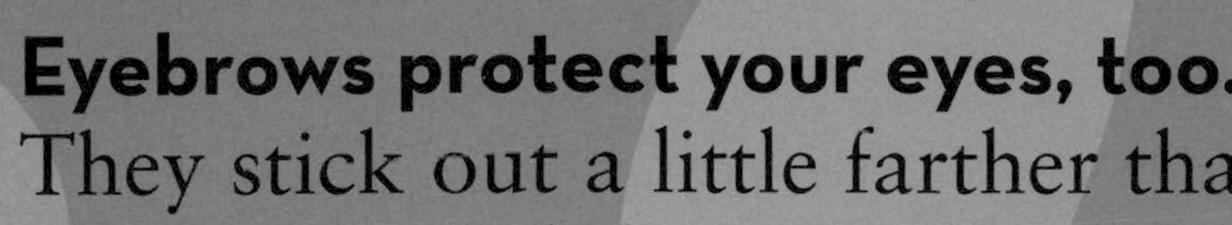

Eyebrows protect your eyes, too. They stick out a little farther than your eyes, and they are shaped in a way that makes sweat and rain flow toward the sides of your face, rather than running into your eyes.

We humans also use our eyebrows to express emotions such as surprise or worry. We keep our eyebrows busy.

Most PEOPLE have 250 to 500 HAIRS in each EYEBROW. But some people can have more than 1,000.

WHY DO I CRY?

Our eyes are constantly making tears. They wash over our eyeballs each time we blink. Those tears help keep our eyes healthy.

BABIES often **CRY** when they're **HUNGRY** or when they need a **DIAPER** change.

Sad feelings can make us cry, too. So can happy or hurt or angry feelings. Any strong feeling might cause our brain to turn on the tears. If we have too many tears for our eyes to hold, they spill over.

Gritty dust, smoke in the air, or even a stray eyelash can make our eyes "water," too. Those tears try to wash our eyes clean.

SOME people **CRY** while chopping an **ONION.** The **TEARS** are caused by a **STRONG NATURAL CHEMICAL** in the onion that **STINGS** our **EYES.**

WHY DOES MY STOMACH GROWL WHEN I'M HUNGRY?

Guess what? Your stomach growls all the time! Working to digest all the food you eat is a full-time job!

Inside your digestive system, food and liquids are broken down to be used by your body. Gas and air bubbles get mixed in, too. And those get noisy!

Gurgle-glurble-growwwl.

Shh, listen. Hear any noises coming from your stomach? If not, there is probably still food in there from the last time you ate. Food muffles, or softens, your stomach's digestive sounds, kind of like a pillow held over a ringing phone.

FACTS

Your stomach is located above your belly button, on the left side of your body.

Your stomach is shaped like a pear.

Food reaches your stomach about seven seconds after you swallow it.

What makes your mouth water?

HOW DOES MY MOUTH WATER?

When you smell good food, saliva—or spit—springs from areas inside your mouth. That is how your mouth prepares to eat. The saliva helps melt chewed food and makes it easier to swallow.

That **GLOB** of **FOOD** and **SPIT** you're about to **SWALLOW** has a name: **BOLUS** (say BO-lus).

WHY DO I BURP?

FOODS especially good at making us **GASSY** are **BEANS, DAIRY PRODUCTS, FIZZY DRINKS,** some **RAW VEGGIES,** and **MEATS.**

When you swallow food and liquids, you also swallow air. That air—plain old air—has gases in it like nitrogen and oxygen.

We pat BABIES on their BACKS to help GAS BUBBLES RISE out of their LITTLE BODIES.

Down in your stomach live billions of bacteria. They help digest your food. They release their own gases.

Some of those gases hanging around inside of you need to come out again. Some push up through the tube connecting your stomach to your throat. And you burp. Excuse you!

Other gases get stuck and move all the way through your digestive system to come popping out the other end. *Pffft!* Excuse you again!

WHY DO I SNEEZE?

SNEEZES send **SPIT** and tiny **PARTICLES** flying out of your **NOSE** and **MOUTH** at nearly **100** miles an hour (161 km/h).

The world is filled with tiny particles that can make you sneeze. Floating in the air are plant pollens, dust, and even flakes of dry skin or hair from animals. When a particle gets up inside your nose and parks itself on the tiny hairs there, watch out.

Your brain feels that particle the moment it lands and wants to blast it OUT. One second you feel a tickle up inside your nose, and the next, your body releases a powerful ah-CHOO!

Why do you think you should cover your mouth when you sneeze?

Many people also sneeze when leaving a dimly lit space and moving into bright sunlight. Scientists say the sunlight somehow causes two or three sneezes in a row.

LET'S PLAY A GAME!

Can you match the pictures to the words that describe what the person is doing?

1

SINGING

RUNNING

SHIVERING

LAUGHING

YAWNING

CRYING

SNEEZING

2

ANSWERS: 1. RUNNING, 2. SHIVERING, 3. SINGING, 4. YAWNING , 5. LAUGHING, 6. SNEEZING, 7. CRYING

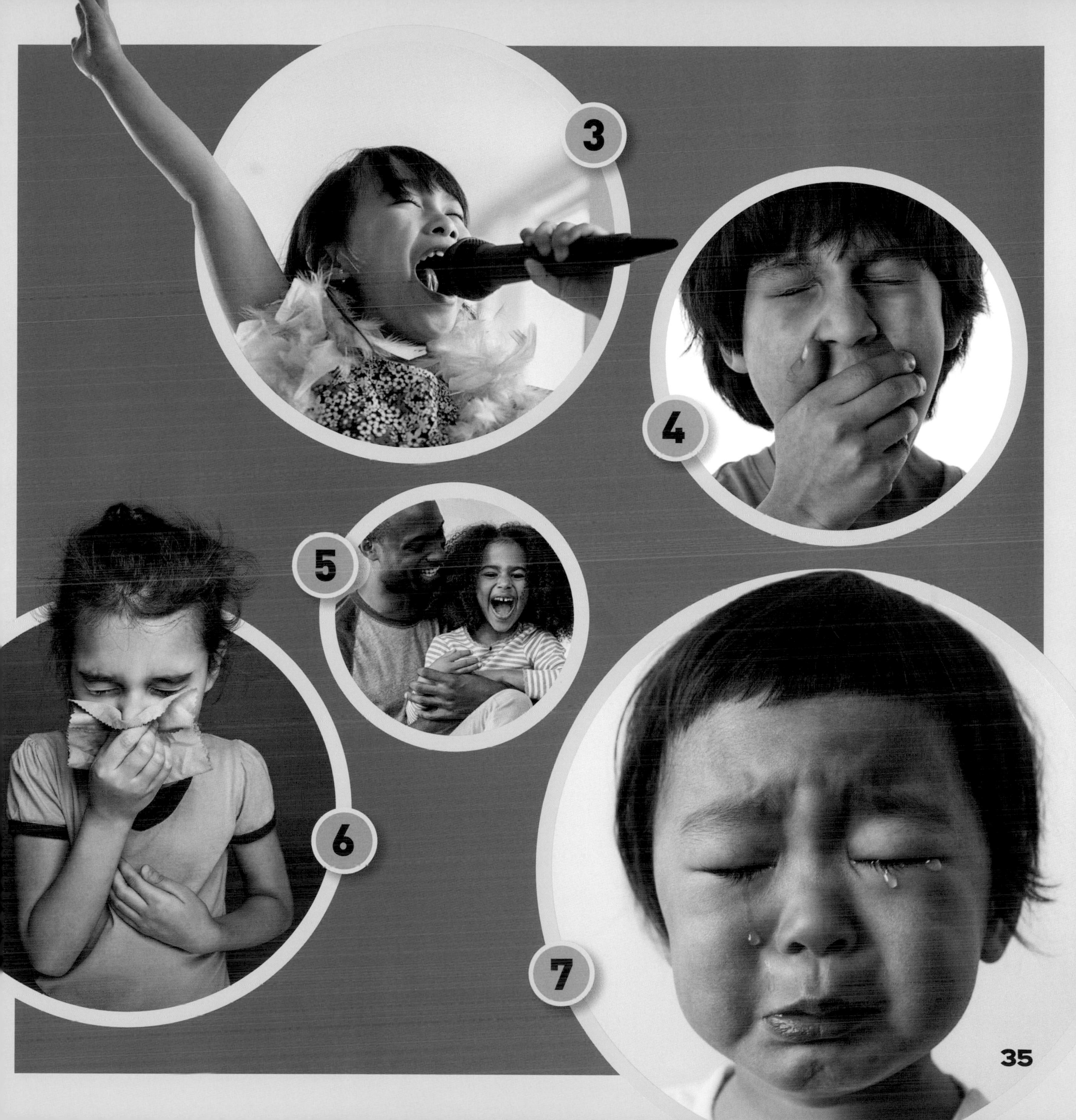
3
4
5
6
7

CHAPTER 2
FUN AND GAMES

Taking time out for fun—to play a game, dance, or simply blow shiny bubbles—is more than a good time. Scientists say playing actually makes us happier and healthier!

WHY DOES MUSIC MAKE ME MOVE?

A part of your brain called the cerebellum (say sare-uh-BELL-um) helps control body movement. When your cerebellum feels a pleasing musical beat, you may want to tap your toes or rock back and forth—or even jump out of your chair to dance, dance, dance!

FACTS

The music you listen to can slow or speed up your heartbeat.

Music may make you more creative.

Athletes perform better to music they enjoy.

Certain types of music make flowers grow faster.

The **PATTERN** of **BEATS** and **SOUNDS** in **MUSIC** is called **RHYTHM** (say RIH-thum).

Human **BRAINS** release a special **CHEMICAL** that makes us **FEEL HAPPY.** Can you guess one thing that starts a **GUSH** of that chemical? **YES, MUSIC!**

WHY ARE BUBBLES ALWAYS ROUND?

Bubbles are always round because that's their natural shape. It's the way the bubble and the air around it and the air inside of it push against each other.

WHY ARE SOAP BUBBLES COLORFUL?

Both the inside and the outside of bubbles reflect light, showing us colors. The thicker a bubble's soapy walls, the more colorful!

Just like **SOAP BUBBLES, CHEWING-GUM BUBBLES** are naturally round.

WHY DO BUBBLES POP?

As soon as you blow a bubble, the air starts drying it. As the bubble dries, its walls get thinner. When the walls get too thin, POP!

What do you like about blowing bubbles?

WHY DO KITES HAVE TAILS?

Kites come in all shapes and sizes. When wind pushes against them, they rise up, up, up into the sky. But sometimes they spin wildly or come crashing to the ground.

A tail adds just enough weight to hold a kite steady as the wind pushes it up.

WHAT ARE KITES MADE OF?

People in China began flying kites about 3,000 years ago. Those kites were made from silk. Most modern kites are made from paper, plastic, or a material called ripstop nylon, which doesn't tear easily.

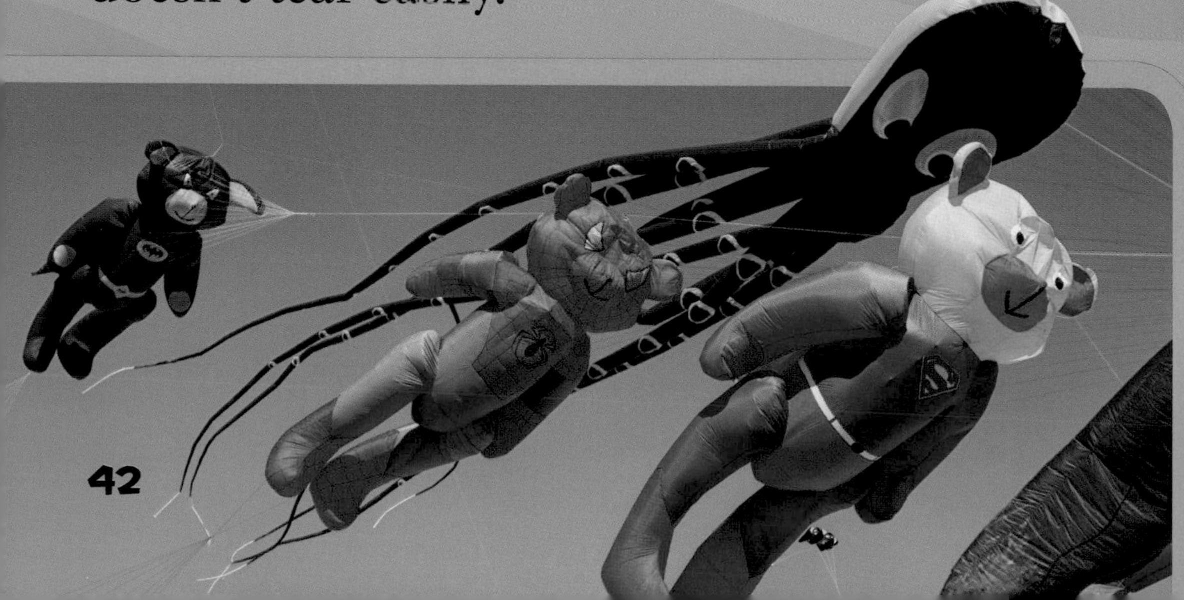

KITE MAKERS often recommend ADDING a TAIL three to eight times the LENGTH of your kite.

A KITE NEEDS a TAIL that is just LONG enough to keep it BALANCED against the WIND. A TOO-SHORT tail won't help at all, and a TOO-LONG tail will make the kite too HEAVY to fly.

What kind of day is best for flying kites?

The **DEEPER** a **POOL** is, the **BLUER** the **WATER** will look.

WHY ARE SWIMMING POOLS BLUE?

To our eyes, light looks white. But it is really made up of many colors. Our eyes just can't see those colors until the light bounces or scatters in certain ways, depending on what the light shines upon.

When light shines through water, its blue color shows up best to our eyes. So an entire pool full of water will always look blue!

WHY DO SOME SWIMMERS WEAR GOGGLES?

Wearing a **CAP** can help **SWIMMERS GLIDE** through the **WATER** faster, so **RACERS** often **WEAR** them.

For people who spend a lot of time in swimming pools, goggles protect their eyes from pool chemicals. Goggles also help swimmers see clearly underwater.

Some swimmers wear caps to keep their hair dry. At some pools, swimmers are asked to wear caps to keep drains from becoming clogged with hair.

WHY DO MARTIAL ARTS HAVE COLORED BELTS?

Students new to martial arts wear white belts. As the students' skills grow, they are given different belts to show that they have passed another level of learning.

One **IMPORTANT** part of learning any **MARTIAL ART** is showing **RESPECT FOR OTHERS** and using **GOOD MANNERS.**

Belt colors stand for things in nature, and students are compared to growing seeds.

2. YELLOW
sunlight shining on the seed

5. BLUE
the blue sky as the plant grows toward it

6. PURPLE
the sky at dawn

7. BROWN
the seed ripens

8. RED
red-hot sun as the plant keeps growing

KARATE, JUDO, and **TAE KWON DO** (say tie-kwon-doh) are all a kind of **MARTIAL ART.**

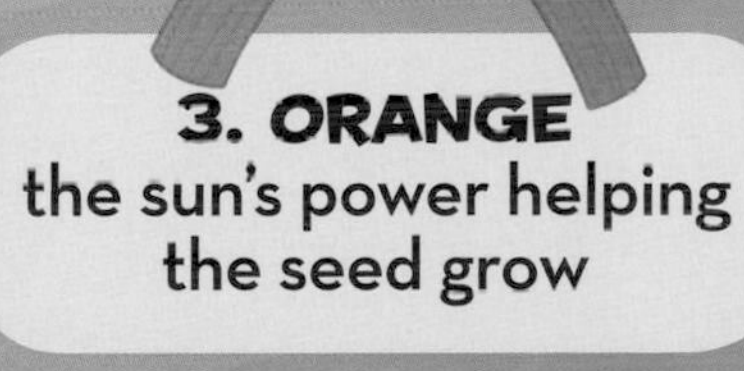

3. ORANGE
the sun's power helping the seed grow

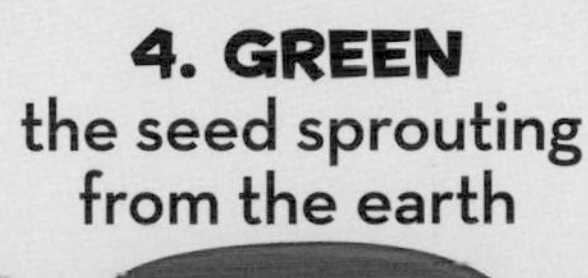

4. GREEN
the seed sprouting from the earth

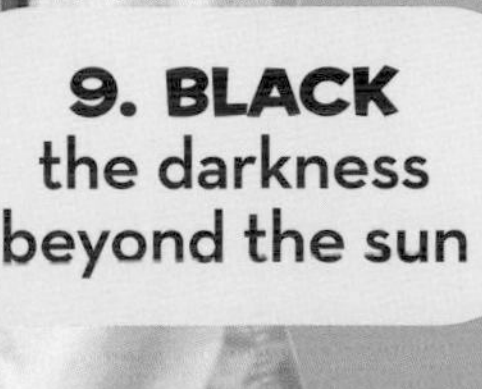

9. BLACK
the darkness beyond the sun

WHY DO BALLS BOUNCE?

When you **BOUNCE** a **BALL HARDER,** it **SQUISHES** even more and bounces back **FASTER** and **HIGHER!**

If you could watch a ball falling in slow motion, you would see it moving down, down, down, then—*smack!*— squishing a bit when it hit the floor. The ball would actually stop, just for a split second, before springing upward and back into its usual round shape.

What kind of balls do you like to play with?

A ball's bounce depends on two important things: how fast it can spring back to its perfect roundness and how hard it hits the floor. But it also depends on what a ball is made of, its size, how much air is inside, and how hard the bouncing surface is.

TRY THIS! BOUNCY, BOUNCY

YOU'LL NEED

five or six balls of various sizes and materials, including one the size of a basketball or soccer ball

1 Hold one of the balls straight out from your chest and let it drop.

2 Do this again with each of the other balls.

3 Which ball bounced highest? Did the ball's size or material matter?

WHY DO REFEREES "TALK" WITH THEIR HANDS?

Some fields of play are large, with players scattered all over the place. Some sports require players to wear protective pads and helmets. Many sports are naturally loud and confusing. It can be tough for players to hear referees, even if they are shouting or blowing a whistle.

For these reasons, referees and umpires in most sports have special hand signals to help players and fans understand what is going on.

Many **REFEREES WEAR UNIFORMS** with **BLACK AND WHITE STRIPES.** This helps them stand out so **PLAYERS** don't **RUN INTO THEM.**

BASKETBALL: PENALTY

BASEBALL: SAFE

Can you invent some hand signals of your own?

SOCCER: WARNING

AMERICAN FOOTBALL: TOUCHDOWN

ICE HOCKEY: PENALTY

WHY CAN'T WE FEED ANIMALS AT THE ZOO?

What animals do you like to watch?

Visitors are not allowed to toss food to lions or monkeys or any other wild animals because that wouldn't be good for the animals. Zookeepers and animal doctors, called veterinarians, are animal experts. Keeping a close eye on what their animals eat—and how much of it—is a very important part of helping animals stay healthy.

PETTING ZOO

Many zoos have areas called petting zoos, where people can get close to and even feed animals like goats, sheep, rabbits, and ponies.

WHY DO ROLLER COASTERS MAKE ME FEEL FUNNY?

Roller coasters are fun! But all that falling and twirling and jerking around can make your stomach feel weird. That's because your insides aren't held tightly in place. So when your body is jerked up and down and around, everything inside you is being bumped and pushed around, too—including your stomach.

WHY DOES SPINNING MAKE ME DIZZY?

Tiny hairs grow along the walls of your ear canals. There's watery fluid in there, too. Together, they control your balance. When you spin, the fluid sloshes around, bending the hairs. The hairs signal to your brain that you are moving.

When you stop spinning, the fluid keeps sloshing against those tiny hairs. That makes your brain think you're still spinning—or even spinning backward. Whoa, I'm dizzy! When the liquid stops sloshing, you feel normal again.

FIGURE SKATERS get **DIZZY,** too! Right after a **SPIN,** they take a few **SLOW STEPS** to **RECOVER** their **BALANCE.**

WHY DOES COTTON CANDY MELT IN MY MOUTH?

Cotton candy is made from sugar, which dissolves, or melts, when it gets wet. That's why the fluffy stuff melts soon after it goes into your mouth. It's wet in there!

To make cotton candy, sugar is heated until it melts. Then the melted sugar is spun out into long threadlike strands that are wrapped onto a stick or paper cone or stuffed into bags. It's fluffy! It's sweet! It's ... gone moments after it hits your tongue.

COTTON CANDY is also called **FAIRY FLOSS.**

TRY THIS! DISSOLVING SUGAR

YOU'LL NEED

one glass of cold water and one glass of hot water, both with the same amount (have an adult help you with this)

a spoon

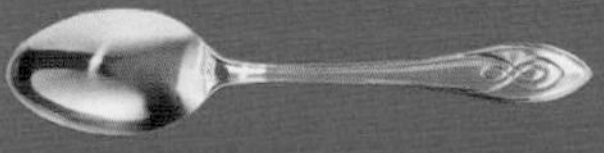

sugar cubes

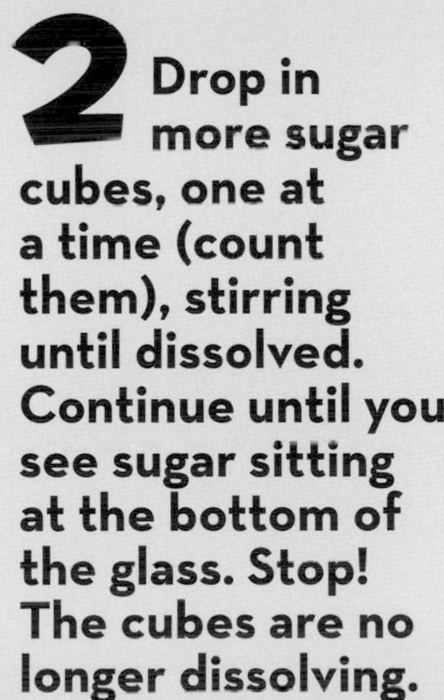

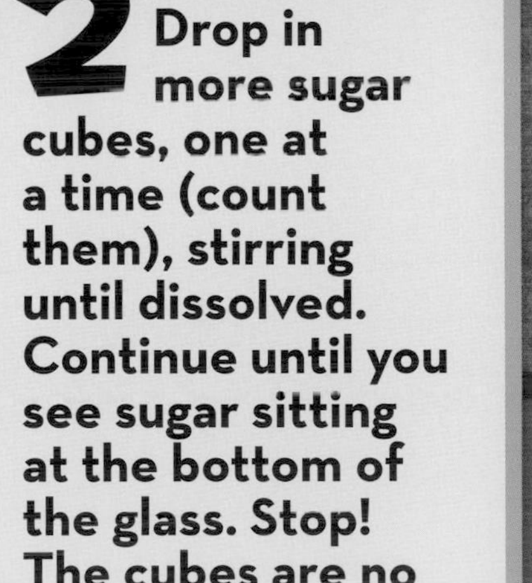

1 Drop a sugar cube into cold water and stir it with the spoon until it dissolves.

2 Drop in more sugar cubes, one at a time (count them), stirring until dissolved. Continue until you see sugar sitting at the bottom of the glass. Stop! The cubes are no longer dissolving.

3 How many sugar cubes completely dissolved in the cold water? Write that number down.

4 Now do the same thing, but drop the sugar cubes into the hot water. Write down the number of cubes that completely dissolved.

Which dissolved more sugar cubes, the hot water or the cold water?

WHY ARE FIREWORKS SO LOUD?

A booming fireworks show is a great way to celebrate holidays and other special times. But the noise can make dogs whine, send cats into hiding, and start babies crying. Fireworks are loud because each firework is an actual explosion.

Where have you seen fireworks?

Firework makers pour an exploding powder into the bottom of a cardboard container shaped like an ice-cream cone. Tiny balls filled with chemical and metal powders go into the top part of the cone. Those top-of-the-cone powders are what creates a firework's colors, sparkles, and BOOMS.

LIGHT travels **FASTER** than **SOUND,** so you'll see a **FIREWORK'S FLASH** of **COLOR** before you **HEAR** its **BOOM.**

FACTS

Fireworks were invented in China more than 2,000 years ago.

Most of the world's fireworks are made in China.

The hardest color to make is blue.

LET'S PLAY A GAME!

A pattern is something that repeats. The balls in each row of this game make a different pattern. Can you say which ball comes next in the pattern in each row?

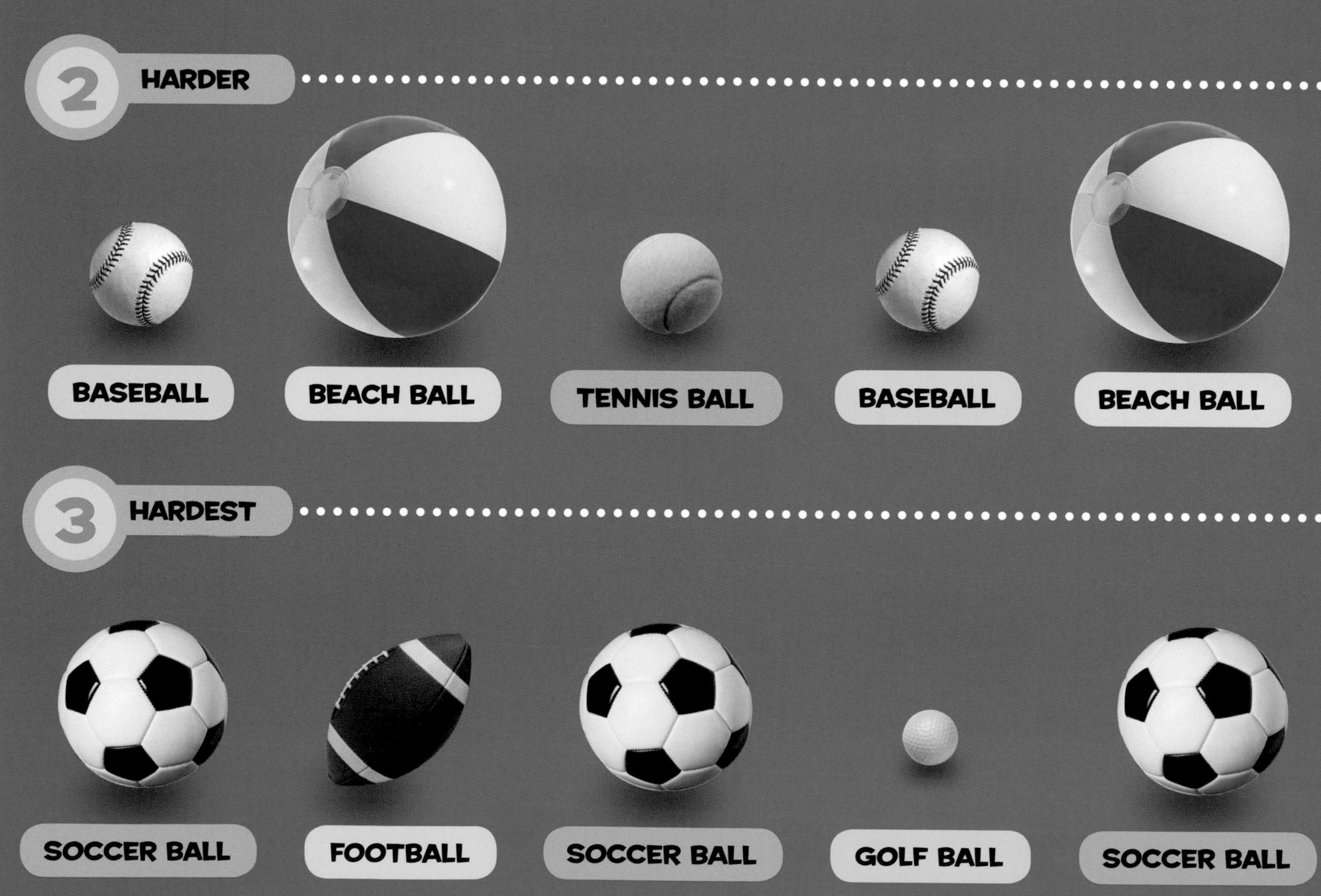

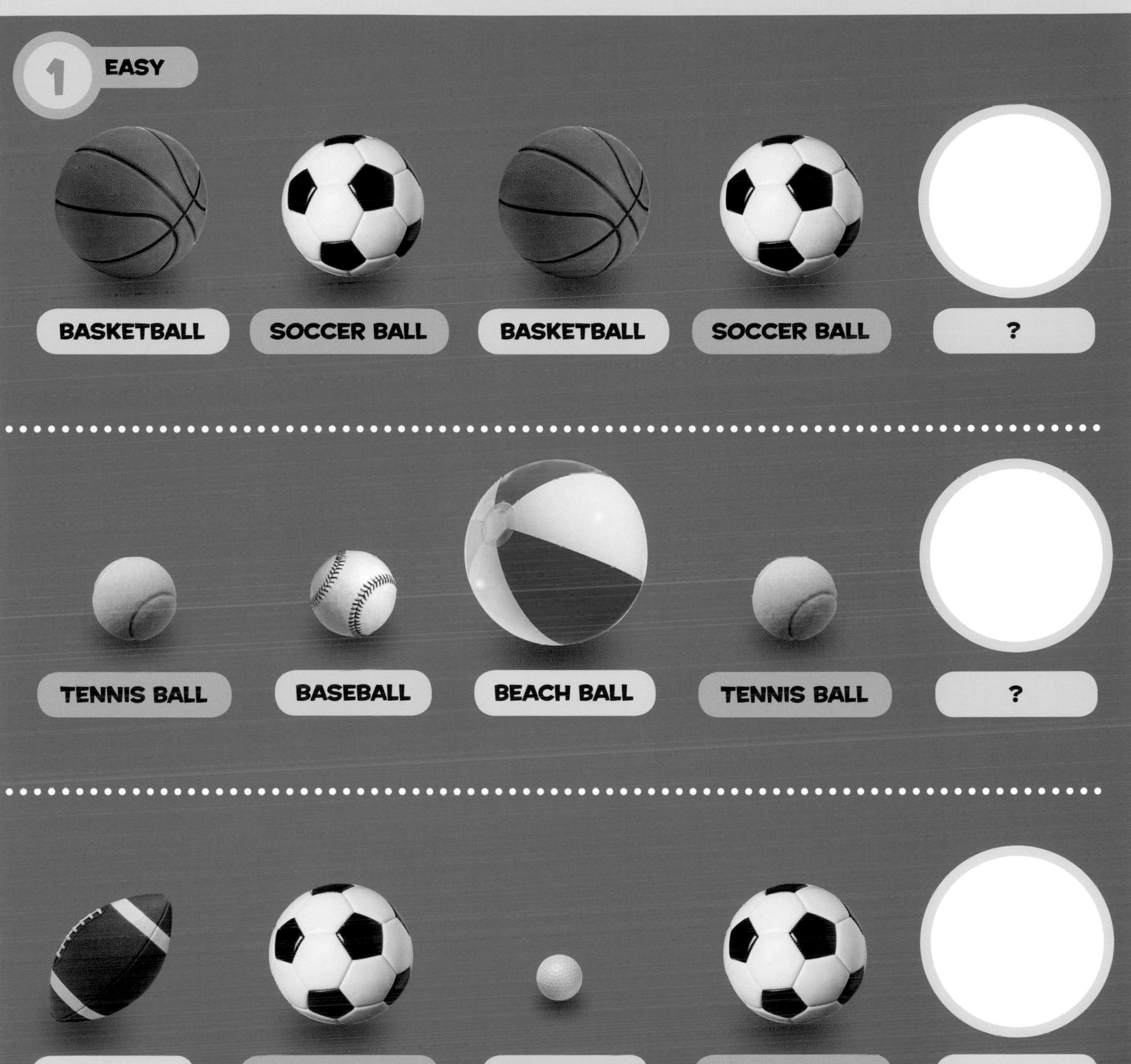
1
EASY
BASKETBALL
SOCCER BALL
BASKETBALL
SOCCER BALL
?
TENNIS BALL
BASEBALL
BEACH BALL
TENNIS BALL
?
FOOTBALL
SOCCER BALL
GOLF BALL
SOCCER BALL
?

CHAPTER 3
AWESOME ANIMALS

Animals swim underwater, burrow underground, swing through trees, and fly in the sky. They're everywhere! They're also fascinating—and full of surprises.

WHY DO DOGS SNIFF EVERYTHING?

Your nose has about six million "smelling cells" that send signals to your brain. But a dog's nose has 300 million of them! No wonder their noses never stop sniff-sniff-sniffing. It's how they explore and understand the world.

A DOG'S NOSTRILS work apart from one another. That means dogs can RECOGNIZE TWO DIFFERENT SMELLS at the same time. They can even WIGGLE each nostril separately.

When dogs meet, sniffing each other is their way of saying hello. Sniffing lets each dog know the age of the other, whether it is male or female, what it has been eating, and even if the other dog is in a good mood!

DOGS have good HEARING, too. They can hear HIGH-PITCHED sounds people cannot.

TRY THIS! TEST YOUR SNIFFER

How good is your nose at recognizing familiar smells? Have an adult help you gather items from around your home like a banana, coffee, chocolate, pencil shavings, cheese, vanilla, an orange, soap … whatever has a strong smell.

Now have the adult tie a blindfold over your eyes. Have them hold each item under your nose, one at a time, while you guess what it is. The adult can write down whether or not you guessed correctly. How many times were you right?

WHY DO A CAT'S EYES SHINE AT NIGHT?

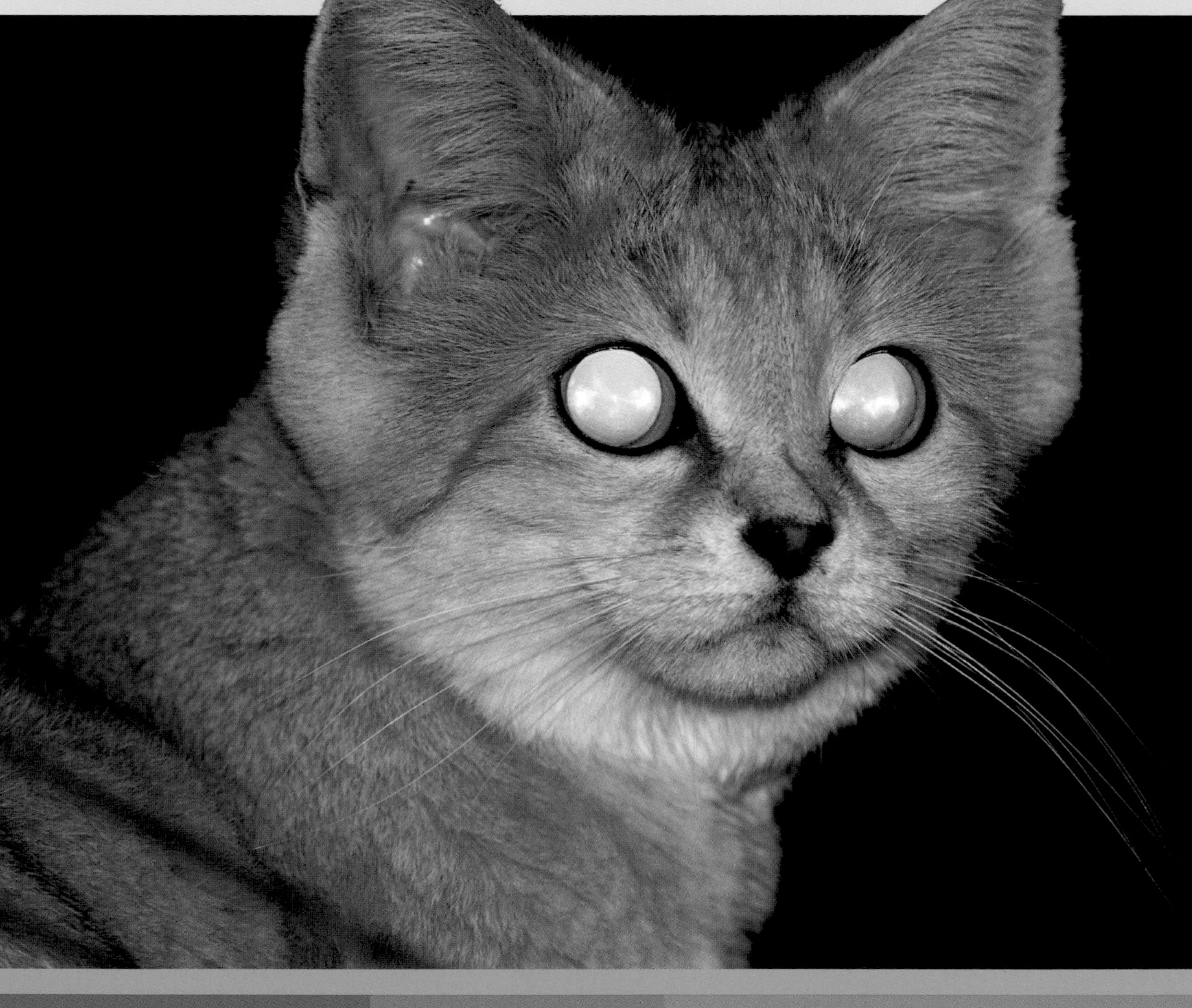

FACTS

- **All animals in the cat family eat meat.**
- **All cats can move silently.**
- **All cats can swim, even though most house cats would rather not.**
- **Cats have excellent night vision.**

You step from the bright hallway into your dark bedroom and are startled to see two glowing eyes under your bed! You know it's just your cat. But what makes its eyes glow like that?

Depending on the type of animal, **LIGHT** may make its **EYES** seem to **GLOW BLUE, GREEN, GOLD, PURPLE, RED,** or **TURQUOISE.**

A cat's eyes do not shine unless light—even dim light—shines into them. The light bounces off a thin reflective layer at the back of its eyes, making the eyes seem to glow. You may have seen the same thing happen when a cat glances in the direction of a car's headlights or into a flashlight's beam.

Other animals with **LIGHT-REFLECTING EYES** are **CATTLE, DEER, DOGS, FERRETS,** and **HORSES.**

WHY DO SOME ANIMALS LIVE UNDERGROUND?

Deserts can be super hot during the day. The sun blazes down, and there's very little shade. So, many desert animals spend their days resting in cool, underground burrows. They come out at night to find food.

Animals that **LOOK FOR FOOD AT NIGHT** are called **NOCTURNAL.**

Burrowing **OWLS LIVE UNDERGROUND** in the **DESERT.**

PRAIRIE DOG

PRAIRIE DOGS live **UNDERGROUND,** but they come **ABOVEGROUND** to look for **FOOD.**

But underground homes aren't just for desert animals. Many animals in forests and woods and meadows and even your backyard live in underground burrows, dens, and tunnels. Under the ground may be the best place for them to rest safely, store food, and raise their young.

Animals like **MOLES** and **WORMS** rarely leave their **DARK, UNDERGROUND** homes. Everything they need to survive is down there.

EARTHWORM

What do you think it would feel like to live underground?

WHY DO MONKEYS LIVE IN TREES?

FACTS

A group of monkeys is called a troop.

Monkeys have tails. Apes do not.

Monkeys can grab things with their fingers AND their toes.

The loudest monkeys, called howler monkeys, have a call that can be heard from three miles (5 km) away.

Animals that spend **MOST** or **ALL** of their **TIME IN TREES** are called **ARBOREAL.**

Many types of monkeys and apes live in trees. Some kinds spend their lives up in the branches. They munch on the berries, fruits, nuts, and seeds of the trees. They eat the insects, lizards, and bird eggs they find there.

Some monkeys have long fingers or sharp claws to help them grip branches. Some monkeys have long tails that work like an extra hand to help them hold on. Still others have powerful legs to help them jump from branch to branch.

Monkeys feel safer in trees, too. High above the ground, they are less likely to come face-to-face with a big jungle cat that wants to eat them.

Can you name some other animals that live in trees?

WHY ARE SOME ANIMALS SO COLORFUL?

Some animals blend into their surroundings so well that they are hard to see. That helps them hide from animals that might want to eat them.

PALE CRACKER BUTTERFLY

If animals do not blend in, it is usually because they don't need to. Their bright colors remind other animals to leave them alone because they might sting or spray a stinky liquid. They might taste horrible or even be poisonous!

MONARCH BUTTERFLIES are **BEAUTIFUL,** but they **TASTE YUCKY** to birds. A bird that tries to **EAT ONE** will get **SICK** and never go near another.

POISON DART FROGS are **BRILLIANTLY** colored, but don't get **TOO CLOSE.** Their **SKIN** is poisonous!

MALE BIRDS are usually more **COLORFUL** than females. They are **NOT POISONOUS.** Their colorful **FEATHERS** simply make them more **ATTRACTIVE** to females.

MANDARIN DUCK

WHY DO KANGAROOS HAVE POUCHES?

Only female kangaroos have pouches. It's where they keep their babies safe and warm. A baby kangaroo is called a joey. When it is born, it is about the size of a jelly bean. Right after it is born, it crawls into its mother's pouch.

After about four months in the pouch, a young joey will sometimes pop out to snack on grass and shrubs. But it won't leave the pouch for good until it is about 10 months old.

Can you hop like a kangaroo?

Marsupials are animals that **CARRY THEIR BABIES** in **POUCHES,** like **KANGAROOS.** Other marsupials include **KOALAS, WOMBATS,** and **OPOSSUMS.**

WHY DO MOOSE HAVE ANTLERS?

A male moose's antlers make him look handsome and healthy to a female moose.

Antlers are part of a moose's skull. Each spring they begin growing up from two bumps on top of the moose's head. They grow and grow all through summer. They stop growing in autumn, and then they fall off. When spring comes around, new ones grow in again. A moose grows a bigger pair of antlers each year.

FACTS

Moose belong to the deer family.

Moose eat grass, leaves, and moss.

They are excellent swimmers.

Moose babies are called calves.

Other animals with antlers include **DEER, ELK,** and **CARIBOU.** Both **MALE** and **FEMALE** caribou grow antlers.

WHY DO BATS FLY AT NIGHT?

Bats fly at night because that's when the insects they like to eat are most active. Bats can't see very well in the dark. But they don't need to. They have a special skill that helps them find insects on the move. It's called echolocation.

While flying, a bat sends out sounds too high-pitched for humans to hear. The way those sounds bounce off buildings, trees, or flying insects tells the bat where the objects are. That's echolocation. The bat can then swoop in and grab the insect. Chomp!

One reason **BATS SLEEP UPSIDE DOWN** is that it's **EASIER** for them to just let go and **FLY AWAY** from that position.

TRY THIS! FIND THAT MOTH!

1 Pretend you are a bat, and your friend is a moth. Tie on your blindfold. Then have your friend stand somewhere across the room.

YOU'LL NEED

cloth to use as a blindfold

a small, empty box

a friend or adult

2 Now make one bat-like squeak. After your squeak, your friend should tap the box once, very softly. Squeak, tap. Squeak, tap. Let your ears guide you closer and closer to your friend until you find him. Then, let your friend be the bat, and you be the moth.

3 The softer the taps, the tougher it will be to find that moth. Try having the moth move around while tapping. Does that make it easier or harder to find him?

WHY DO FIREFLIES GLOW?

At nighttime, male fireflies fly around flashing to attract females. Female fireflies wait in the grass below or on other plants. When they see a flash pattern they like, they flash back to let males know where they are.

Fireflies make a special chemical in their abdomens that glows when air touches it. Through small holes in its abdomen, a firefly lets in a bit of air, then cuts it off. That makes its light flash on, off, on, off.

There are more than 2,000 KINDS of FIREFLIES. Each kind has its own FLASH PATTERN.

Fireflies are also called **LIGHTNING BUGS.**

Fireflies are **WARM WEATHER INSECTS.** You might see them in the **WOODS,** in **BACKYARDS,** above **FARM FIELDS,** and just about anywhere **PLANT LIFE** is **GREEN** and **GROWING.**

Have you ever seen fireflies glowing in the dark?

AWESOME ANIMALS

Here are some other animals that shine their own light.

LANTERNFISH

WARTY COMB JELLYFISH

FIREFLY SQUID

WHY DO SKUNKS STINK?

A skunk does not stink unless it is frightened by another animal or a human. Then, watch out! To defend itself, it shoots an oily, superstinky spray from under its tail. Pee-yew! But it doesn't spray without first giving a few warnings. It wiggles to show its black and white colors. It dances in place. It thumps the ground with its feet.

If the other animal still won't leave it alone, the skunk sprays. The spray burns the eyes of the animal. It stings the inside of the animal's nose. Ow! While the animal is hurting and upset, the skunk has time to run away.

If you see a **SKUNK, GIVE IT** plenty of **ROOM.** Its **SPRAY** can shoot **10 FEET (3 M)!**

When a **STINK BUG** is **AFRAID,** it leaks out a **STINKY, BAD-TASTING LIQUID** to keep other animals from eating it.

When another animal **FRIGHTENS A VULTURE,** the vulture **THROWS UP.** The **STINK** is usually enough to make the **SCARY ANIMAL** back off.

Can you name some other stinky smells?

WHY DON'T PENGUINS GET COLD?

Not all penguins live in cold places. But the ones that do are perfectly suited to that refrigerated life.

Penguins have **LEATHERY, WEBBED FEET**—just right for standing on **ICE.**

How do you keep warm?

The **LARGEST PENGUIN** is the **EMPEROR PENGUIN.** It is about as **TALL** as a **FIRST-GRADE KID.**

Emperor penguins live in icy, snowy Antarctica. Their feathers are tiny and packed so tightly that they are waterproof. Under the feathers is a thick layer of fat called blubber that helps a penguin stay warm.

When penguins do get cold, they huddle together in a huge crowd. They take turns rotating in and out of the cozy, warm middle.

WHY DO WALRUSES HAVE SUCH LONG TUSKS?

A walrus is a graceful swimmer. But hauling its enormous body up out of the water is hard. That's where those long front teeth, called tusks, come in handy. Walruses hook their tusks on to the edge of the ice and pull. A walrus also uses its tusks to break breathing holes into the ice from below.

TUSKS are always growing. An older **WALRUS'S** tusks might be **THREE FEET** (1 m) **LONG!**

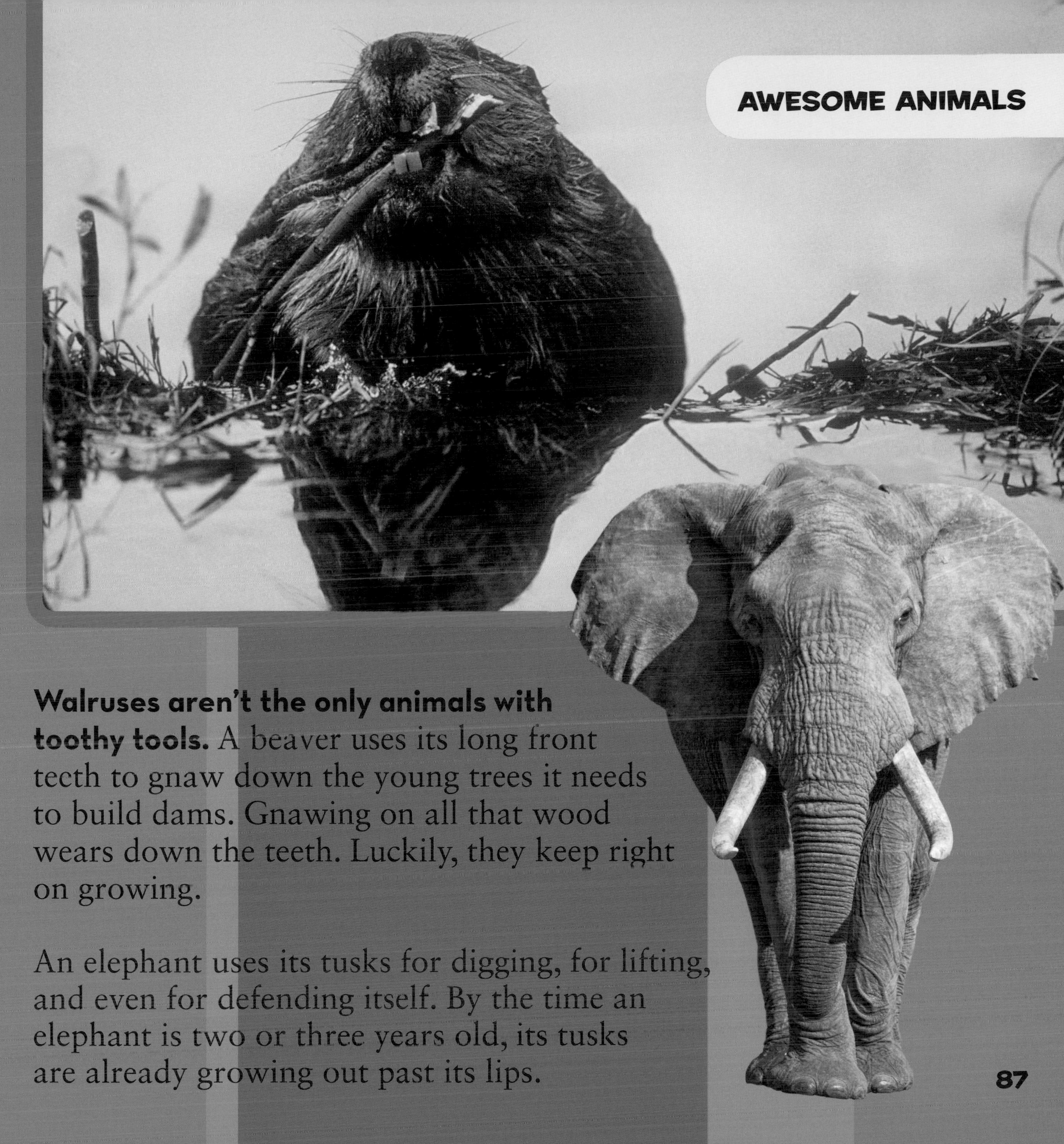

Walruses aren't the only animals with toothy tools. A beaver uses its long front teeth to gnaw down the young trees it needs to build dams. Gnawing on all that wood wears down the teeth. Luckily, they keep right on growing.

An elephant uses its tusks for digging, for lifting, and even for defending itself. By the time an elephant is two or three years old, its tusks are already growing out past its lips.

WHY DO WOLVES LIVE IN PACKS?

Wolves have a better chance of survival when they hunt in a pack. Hunting together makes it easier to take down large animals like moose and elk. Alone, a wolf wouldn't eat very well.

But easier hunting isn't the only reason wolves live in packs. Each pack is a family made up of two parents and their baby wolves, called pups, of all ages. They do everything together. That includes making time for play!

All the adults help feed and protect the pups. For almost three months, the pups stay in the den. When pack members leave to hunt for food, one wolf stays behind to babysit the pups until they're big enough to stay alone or join the hunt.

FACTS

Wolves live in packs of 3 to 20 members.

Wolves are members of the dog family.

A wolf pack may travel up to 30 miles (48 km) in one day.

Wolves eat large animals like deer, elk, and sheep. They also hunt birds, fish, squirrels, and snakes.

WOLVES COMMUNICATE by barking, whining, growling, **YIPPING, WOOFING,** and **HOWLING.**

Sometimes a **WOLF** will begin **HOWLING** simply because it **HEARS** another wolf howling.

Can you howl like a wolf?

WHY DO BIRDS SING?

Mockingbirds can **COPY** the **SONGS OF OTHER BIRDS.** They can even **COPY** a **CAT'S MEOW** or a **FROG'S CROAK!**

Birds whose singing is pleasant and musical are called songbirds. Scientists think songbirds sing to attract mates. If the singer is male, it may sing to warn other males to stay away from its territory.

Each kind of songbird has its own pattern of whistles and trills. Some songs even sound like words. For example, a chickadee seems to sing *chick-a-deedeedee!* A cardinal seems to sing *cheer, cheer, birdie-birdie-birdie!*

Not all birds are songbirds. Instead of pretty songs, some birds squawk, honk, or caw. Others chirp, screech, whistle, or hoot. Still others cluck, quack, or cock-a-doodle-doo.

Can you make some bird sounds?

TRY THIS! TIME FOR A SONG

YOU'LL NEED

All you need for this experiment is a place to hear birds. You can go outside to do this, or you can stay indoors beside an open window.

1 Find out when the birds in your neighborhood do most of their singing.

2 Listen for birds three times, for five to ten minutes each time. Try it first thing in the morning, at noon, and again just before it gets dark.

3 Did you hear more birds singing early in the morning, in the middle of the day, or just before settling down for the night? Why do you think they did more singing at that time of day?

WHY ARE DINOSAUR NAMES SO LONG?

When a scientist finds the fossilized bones of a never before seen dinosaur, that scientist can name it whatever he or she wants. Since those names often have a "saurus" ending, they can get pretty long.

Some dinosaurs are named for the places where they were discovered. Some dinos are named after the person who discovered them.

The word "dinosaur" combines two Greek words, *deinos* and *sauros*. *Deinos* means "terrible." *Sauros* means "lizard." Ta-da! Terrible lizards.

One of the SHORTEST dinosaur names is MINMI (say MIN-mee).

One of the **SMALLEST** dinosaurs has the **LONGEST** name: *Micropachycephalosaurus* (say MY-cro-PACK-ee-SEF-ah-lo-SORE-us). **WHEW!**

If you could name a newly discovered dinosaur, what would you call it?

LET'S PLAY A GAME!

What in the world are these animals?

7

8

9

10

11

12

ANSWERS: 1. WOLF, 2. CAT, 3. OWL, 4. MONKEY, 5. BUTTERFLY, 6. FROG, 7. MOOSE, 8. BAT, 9. SKUNK, 10. PENGUIN, 11. WALRUS, 12. DINOSAUR

CHAPTER 4
NATURE ALL AROUND

From oceans to puddles, from sunsets to seeds ... our Earth is filled with wonders. Aren't we lucky to live here?

WHY IS OCEAN WATER SO SALTY?

Most of the salt in the world's oceans got there from rocks on land. How? Falling rain slowly breaks down rocks, then washes their salty minerals into streams and rivers. Rivers carry them to the sea.

WHY CAN'T I DRINK OCEAN WATER?

Ocean water has too much salt for your body to handle. Instead of making thirsty people feel better, drinking ocean water makes them sick.

DO FISH DRINK OCEAN WATER?

Fish do drink ocean water, but they have special body parts—their gills and kidncys—that remove most of the salt.

OCEAN CREATURES without gills—like **DOLPHINS, SEALS,** and **WHALES**—can't drink ocean water. Instead **THEY GET WATER FROM THE FOODS THEY EAT,** like fish and squid.

WHY DOES FOG FEEL WET?

If you've ever been outside on a foggy day, then you've been in a cloud! Fog is nothing more than a cloud that forms at ground level. It is made of water droplets so tiny and light they float in the air. When you are in fog, you can feel the wetness on your skin.

Do you have foggy days where you live?

FOG can be so **THICK** that you **CAN'T SEE THROUGH IT.**

WHY IS GRASS WET IN THE MORNING?

Sometimes, even when it hasn't been raining, you step onto grass in the morning and end up with wet feet or shoes. Those tiny water droplets clinging to blades of grass are called dew. They form when a warm, sunny day is followed by a cool, clear night.

Dew also forms on spiderwebs, low shrubs and flowers, and even slow-moving insects!

WHY DO PUDDLES DISAPPEAR?

Rain leaves behind puddles of water. They're fun to splash in, but they quickly disappear. Where did that water go?

When the sun comes out after a rain, it shines on a puddle. That warms the water. As the water heats up, it changes—from water into invisible water vapor. The vapor is so light that it rises into the air. That is called evaporation.

Eventually, water vapor up in the air forms into tiny droplets. Those droplets huddle together to form clouds, and you know what clouds can bring—more rain!

Millions of **TEENY WATER DROPLETS** come together to make **ONE** raindrop.

TRY THIS! WHERE'D THE WATER GO?

YOU'LL NEED

two clear plastic cups

plastic wrap

a marker

a rubber band

paper and a pencil

1 Fill the cups half full of water, the same amount in each.

2 Cover one cup with plastic wrap and secure with a rubber band. Leave the other uncovered.

3 Set the cups side by side in a sunny place. Use a marker to mark the water line in each cup.

4 Every day or so, look at the cups to see if the water level has changed. If it goes down, the water is evaporating!

5 Which cup does the water evaporate faster in? Does anything form on the plastic in the covered cup?

WHY DOES SUNSHINE FEEL HOT?

The sun is a giant ball of fiery gases. The temperature at its surface is nearly 10,000°F (5500°C)! All that heat has to go somewhere. One of those places is Earth.

It takes sunlight eight minutes to reach our planet. By that time, it has cooled enough to make life possible. But it's still strong enough to feel hot on our tender human skin.

WHY CAN'T I LOOK AT THE SUN?

Looking at the sun—even when that brightness is reflected off sand, snow, or water—can burn the thin outer layer of our delicate eyeballs. Stay safe: Wear sunglasses.

Why do you think it feels cooler in the shade?

WHY DOES MY SHADOW CHANGE SHAPE?

You're outside on a sunny day, and you notice that you don't have much of a shadow. Yet later in the afternoon, your shadow is super long and skinny. Why did it change?

It isn't because your body suddenly shrank or grew. It's because the sun is shining down from a different place in the sky. You just happen to be standing so that your body blocks the sunlight shining at the ground. That's what creates a shadow.

If the sun is low in the sky, your shadow will be long. If the sun is right above your head, you won't have much of a shadow at all.

TRY THIS! SHIFTING SHADOWS

Try this experiment to see how light shining from different angles changes the shape of a shadow.

YOU'LL NEED

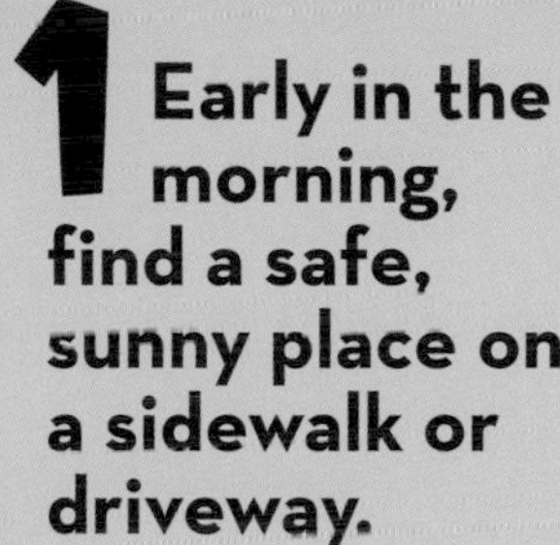

- a large sheet of paper
- a pencil
- a plastic bottle or jug filled with water

1 Early in the morning, find a safe, sunny place on a sidewalk or driveway.

2 Place the bottle or jug in the center of the paper. You might want to tape the edges of the paper to the sidewalk.

3 Trace the outline of the bottle's shadow on the paper and write the time beside it.

4 Check the paper every hour or two and retrace the bottle's shadow. How does the shadow change over the day? What time was the shadow the longest?

WHY DO PUMPKINS HAVE SO MANY SEEDS?

One step in turning a pumpkin into a jack-o'-lantern is sticking your arm inside and pulling out its wet, stringy guts. There might be hundreds and hundreds of seeds to remove, too. Why are there so many? Seeds are the pumpkin plant's way of growing more pumpkins.

Take a look at a pumpkin's ribs. Those are the lines that run from the pumpkin's top to its bottom. Inside each of those ribs is a row of seeds. Plant a seed and, with a little rain and some sunshine, it will sprout and grow into a new pumpkin plant.

Pumpkins are a type of **SQUASH.** Squash come in many **SHAPES, SIZES,** and **COLORS**—including **BLUE!**

The number of **SEEDS** in a **PUMPKIN** has nothing to do with its size. **SMALLER PUMPKINS** can have **MORE SEEDS** than larger ones.

What do you like about pumpkins?

WHY ARE THERE SO MANY KINDS OF FLOWERS?

Plants need sunlight and water to grow. But they also need bees, butterflies, and hummingbirds to visit them. As one of these creatures moves around on a flower, powdery yellow stuff called pollen sticks to its body. When it visits the next flower, some pollen falls off.

When one flower's pollen gets on another flower, that second flower can make seeds. Why? So more plants will grow. This is called pollination.

Many different kinds of animals pollinate plants. Flowers have different sizes, shapes, colors, and smells to attract those creatures.

The CORPSE FLOWER SMELLS like ROTTING MEAT. This stink ATTRACTS the plant's favorite POLLINATORS: FLIES.
CAN YOU SEE WHY THESE FLOWERS WERE NAMED ...
MONKEY FACE ORCHID
SWADDLED BABIES ORCHID
FLYING DUCK ORCHID
CORPSE FLOWER

WHY DO WEEDS GROW IN GARDENS?

Planting seeds to grow a garden is fun. But if gardeners aren't careful, weeds can soon take over. That becomes a big problem when the weeds block sunlight and space needed by the flowers and vegetables we want to grow.

Weed seeds can blow into our gardens on the wind. They can be dropped by birds. They can even be hidden in the soil of plants we buy at a garden center or on the bottom of our shoes.

DANDELIONS

Some **WEEDS,** like **DANDELIONS,** can be pretty. They are only called weeds because they **GROW WHERE WE DON'T WANT THEM.**

Where have you seen weeds?

SHEEP and GOATS love to EAT WEEDS.

WHY DO MUSHROOMS GROW ON SOME TREES?

Mushrooms may seem like strange plants, but they are not plants. They are a type of the living things called fungi. Mushrooms get the food they need from things that used to be alive, like rotting plants. That's why we often see them growing on fallen logs or the bark of dying trees.

Mushrooms come in many sizes, shapes, and colors. Scientists believe there are more than 50,000 different kinds of mushrooms on Earth.

FACTS

Scientists say lightning makes some mushrooms grow faster.

Some mushrooms are poisonous.

Some mushrooms glow in the dark.

NATURE ALL AROUND
LION'S MANE
TURKEY TAIL
DO YOU THINK THESE MUSHROOMS LOOK LIKE THEIR NAMES?
PUFFBALL
VEILED LADY

WHY DON'T TREES FALL OVER?

Have you ever seen trees bending and whipping in a strong wind? It seems amazing that they don't fall over! But tree roots are strong. They hold trees in place through all but the most powerful winds.

As a tree grows, its tough roots keep reaching down and out, always seeking the water and food the tree needs. The farther and deeper those roots reach, the better they'll hold the tree.

FACTS

The tallest trees in the world are redwoods growing in Northern California.

Some trees live for thousands of years.

Trees make oxygen that humans and other animals need to breathe.

Do you have a favorite tree?

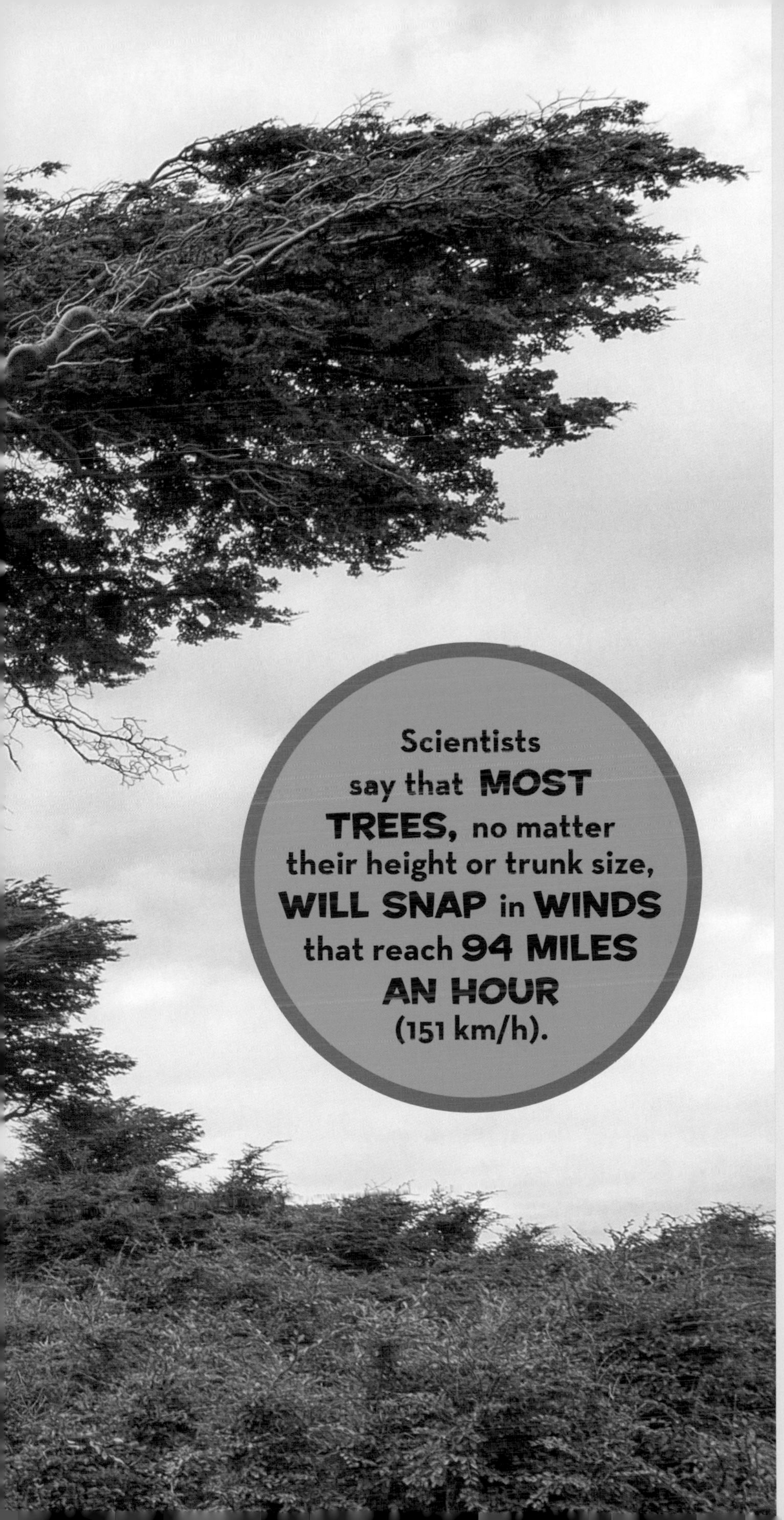

Scientists say that **MOST TREES,** no matter their height or trunk size, **WILL SNAP** in **WINDS** that reach **94 MILES AN HOUR** (151 km/h).

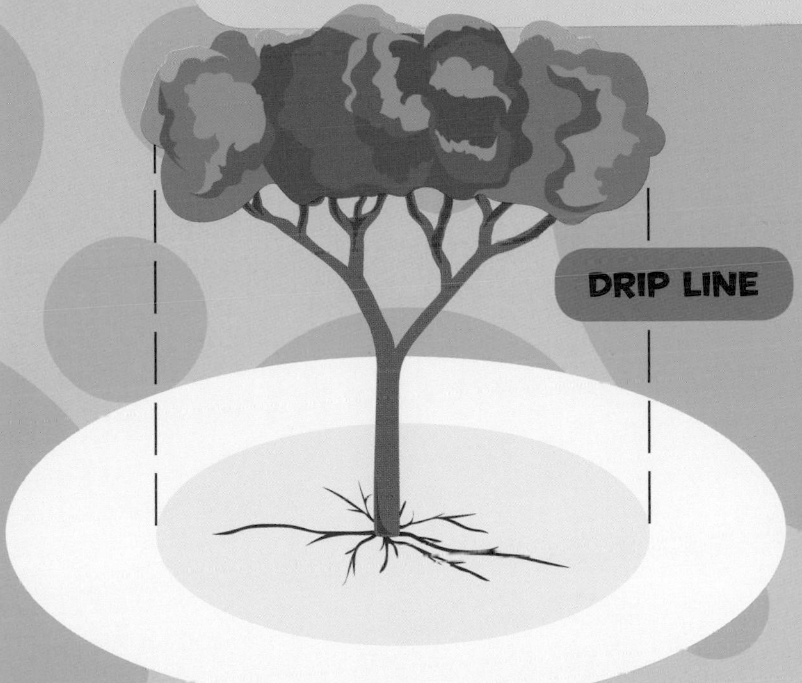

HOW FAR DO ROOTS REACH?

Look at a tree and notice how far out from the trunk its branches grow. Now imagine drawing a circle on the ground under those farthest branch tips. That imaginary circle is called the tree's drip line. See how far it is from one side of the drip line to the other? That tree's root system can reach out even farther.

WHY ARE SOME DESERTS SO HOT AND DRY?

Most **DESERTS** get **LESS THAN 10 INCHES** (25 cm) of **RAIN A YEAR.**

SAHARA, AFRICA

We think of deserts as hot, dry places where rocks and sand stretch as far as our eyes can see. But not every desert is covered with sand, and not every desert is hot. To be called a desert, a place just has to be dry enough.

FACTS

When rain falls above a hot desert, it often dries before reaching the ground.

The world's largest hot desert is the Sahara, in Africa.

Deserts sometimes get quick bursts of rain, then go weeks and weeks without another drop.

CHILE

ULURU, AUSTRALIA
(ALSO CALLED AYERS ROCK)

So why don't hot, dry deserts ever get cool air and refreshing rains? Usually it's because they are in places where weather systems—clouds and storms—don't reach. All that rain gets dropped on other places, and there's no rain left for deserts. With no clouds to block the sunshine, the ground gets blazing hot, and it stays that way.

The **FROZEN CONTINENT** of **ANTARCTICA** is an example of a cold desert.

ANTARCTICA

SUNRISES and SUNSETS can give us AWESOME COLOR SHOWS, spreading REDS, PURPLES, YELLOWS, and ORANGES where the sky meets the ground.

WHY DOES THE SUN RISE AND SET?

It looks like the sun rises in the east early every morning and then goes down, or sets, in the west every evening. Between those times, the sun seems to float slowly along a high path across the sky. But the sun isn't really moving. We are!

The Earth we live on spins all the way around, or rotates, one time every 24 hours. That equals one entire day and night. When the place we live faces the sun, it's our daytime. When the place we live faces away from the sun, say "Nighty night!"

TRY THIS! DAY INTO NIGHT INTO DAY

This experiment will help you understand how Earth rotates. *Be careful not to shine the light in your partner's eyes.*

YOU'LL NEED

a partner

a darkened room—but not totally dark

a flashlight

any ball about the size of a basketball

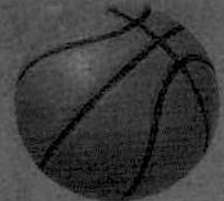

a small sticker of any kind, or a piece of shiny tape

1 Place the sticker anywhere on the ball. Pretend the sticker is you.

2 In a darkened room, have your partner hold the ball up with the sticker facing you.

3 Shine the flashlight at the sticker on the ball. Remember, the flashlight is the sun, so hold it steady.

4 Have your partner slowly spin, or rotate, the ball, until the sticker is on the side away from your flashlight sun.

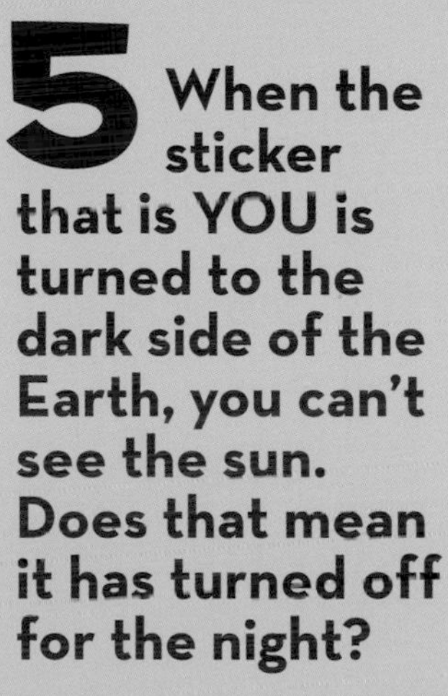

5 When the sticker that is YOU is turned to the dark side of the Earth, you can't see the sun. Does that mean it has turned off for the night?

LET'S PLAY A GAME!

Use the pictures to help you read this story about a garden.

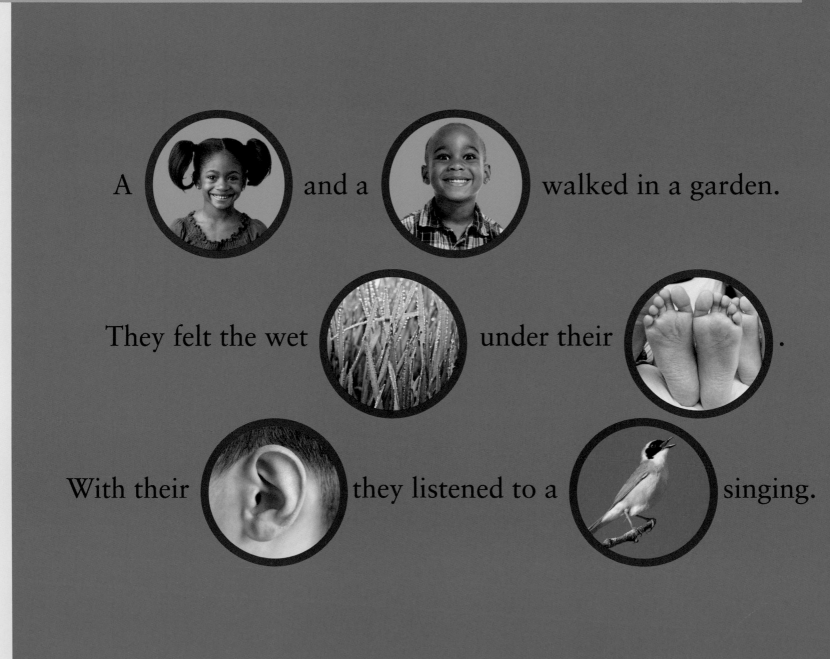

A  and a  walked in a garden.

They felt the wet  under their 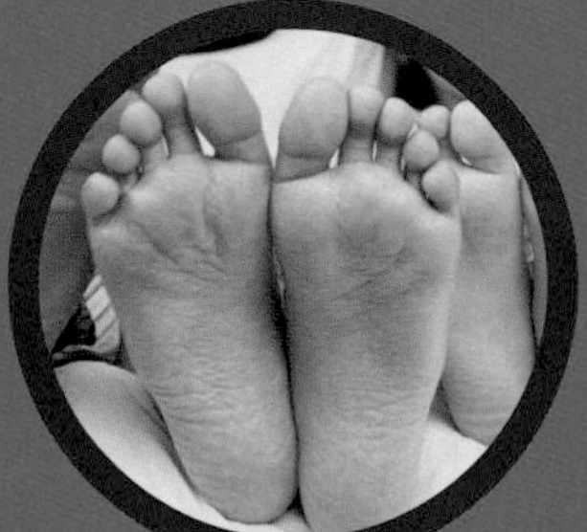.

With their 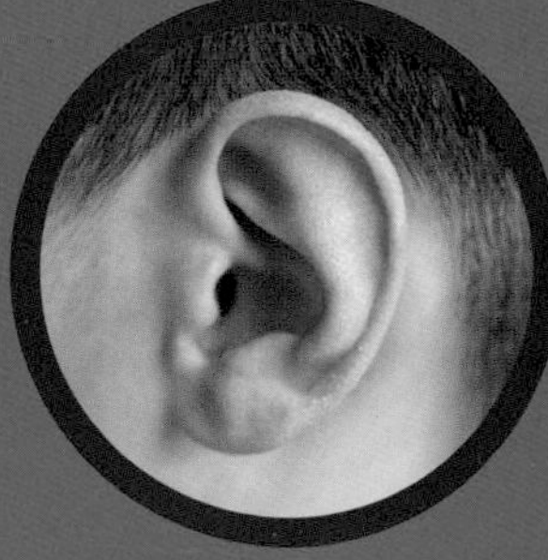 they listened to a  singing.

The children used their 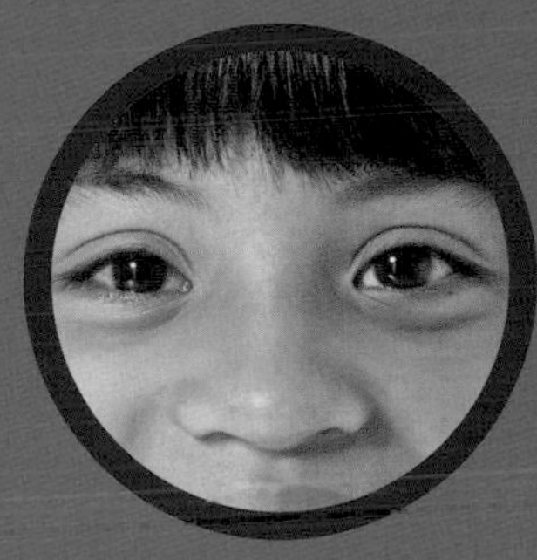

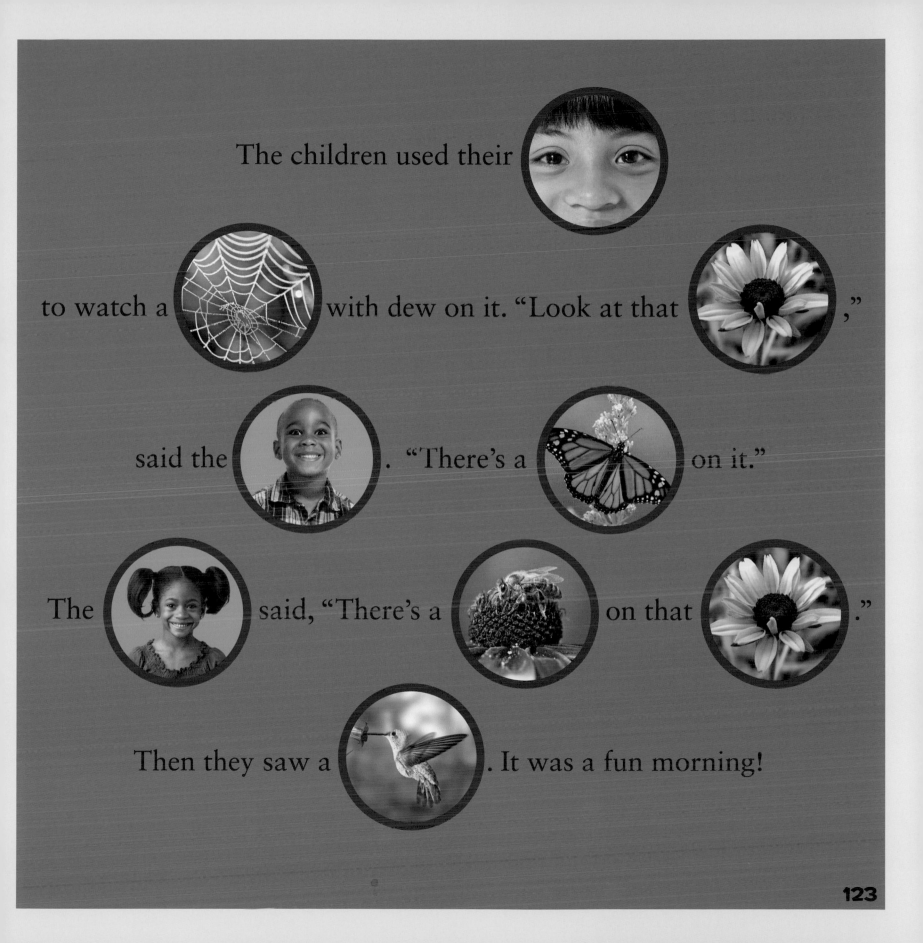

to watch a  with dew on it. "Look at that ,"

said the . "There's a  on it."

The  said, "There's a  on that ."

Then they saw a . It was a fun morning!

PARENT TIPS

Extend your child's experience beyond the pages of this book. Get outside with your child and observe the natural world. Visit libraries, museums, zoos, and farmers markets with your child. Go to concerts and listen to music together. All these things can provide valuable educational opportunities for curious kids, inspiring them to keep asking why. Here are some other activities you can do with National Geographic's *Little Kids First Big Book of Why 2*.

DOGGY DAYS
(PERCEPTION)

Encourage your child to roam your home on all fours, imagining life as a dog. Help her make a list of which everyday actions are easier for a dog than a human and which are harder. What kinds of things do dogs do that humans don't? How would a dog ask for food or playtime?

CONTAGIOUS YAWNING
(EXPERIMENT)

Have your child fake yawn a few times in an effort to trigger a real yawn. Does it work? If so, how many fake yawns did it take? Now allow your child to try to get a yawn out of you (or an unsuspecting relative). Did fake yawning trigger a real yawn? How many fake yawns did it take?

DIGGING THE BEAT
(LISTENING/ EXERCISE)

Play a few minutes of various kinds of music for your child. Ask which rhythms make him feel like tapping toes or jumping up to dance. Encourage him to design a few dance moves. Anything goes!

BUBBLE COLORS
(OBSERVATION)

A soap bubble's surface changes as it dries. Blues and purples give way to shades of oranges and yellows just before a bubble bursts. Have your child blow bubbles, then focus on one to follow its color changes. Can your child predict by its color when a bubble is about to pop?

KANGAROO JUMP
(MEASURING)

Have your child stand at a line, feet together, knees bent, arms held at her sides. Then have her jump forward. Mark the point behind your child's heels, then help her measure the jump. Now tell her to add arm swings to the jump. Measure that distance. Do arm swings help your child jump farther?

FIREFLY FLASHES
(PATTERNS)

Each firefly has its own flash pattern. With two flashlights, sit in a darkened room with your child and flash a simple light pattern toward the ceiling. Can your child repeat it back to you? Take turns initiating various flash patterns. Be careful not to look directly into the flashlight's bright beam.

NAME THAT DINO
(IMAGINATION)

When a new dinosaur is discovered, the finder gets to name it. Have your child pretend to discover a brand-new dinosaur in your backyard or nearby, then have him come up with a name for it. Remind your child that names often include the name of the finder, the location of the discovery, or one of the animal's features.

SONGBIRD SNACK TIME

(CRAFT)

Bring birds to your yard with a simple feeder. You'll need an empty toilet paper roll, peanut butter, and birdseed. (If your child is allergic to peanut butter, use solid vegetable shortening.) Thread a long string through the tube. Help your child spread peanut butter thickly all around the tube. Roll it in birdseed. Hang the tube somewhere outdoors and watch the birds fly in!

PICKING POSIES

(MEMORY)

Create your own cards for a memory game. Paste white paper to cardboard from an empty cereal box, then cut into squares when dry. Draw simple flowers on the cards and color pairs alike. You might draw two flowers with yellow petals, two flowers with blue petals, etc. Then turn the cards upside down, and flip up two at a time, searching for matching flowers.

GLOSSARY

ARBOREAL: having to do with trees

BACTERIA: tiny living things too small for us to see without a microscope

CEREBELLUM: a part of our brain that helps control body movement

DIGESTIVE SYSTEM: a group of body parts, including the stomach, that work to turn food into energy

DISSOLVE: melt away

EVAPORATION: the change of a liquid into an invisible gas called a vapor

FUNGI: a group of living things that are not plants, animals, or bacteria. Mushrooms, molds, yeasts, and mildews are all fungi.

GILL: a special body part that is used for breathing by many animals that live in the water, such as fish

LARYNX: the upper part of the windpipe. The larynx is also called the voice box.

NOCTURNAL: active at night

NOSTRILS: nose openings that humans and many other animals breathe through

RHYTHM: the pattern of beats and sounds in music

TUSKS: long, pointed teeth that stick out past an animal's mouth

WATER VAPOR: water that has turned into an invisible gas that hangs in the air

ADDITIONAL RESOURCES

BOOKS

Boyer, Crispin. *Why?: Over 1,111 Answers to Everything*. National Geographic Kids Books, 2015.

Boyer, Crispin. *Why Not?: Over 1,111 Answers to Everything*. National Geographic Kids Books, 2018.

Esbaum, Jill. *Little Kids First Big Book of How*. National Geographic Kids Books, 2016.

National Geographic Kids. *Weird But True Sports: 300 Wacky Facts About Awesome Athletics*. National Geographic Kids Books, 2016.

Shulman, Mark, and K.C. Kelley. *BIG Book of Why: 1,001 Facts Kids Want to Know*. Time for Kids, 2016.

WEBSITES

A note for parents and teachers: For more information on this topic, you can visit these websites with your young readers.

easyscienceforkids.com

kidshealth.org/en/kids

natgeokids.com

wonderopolis.com

INDEX

Boldface indicates illustrations.

A

Animals 62–95
- antlers 76–77, **76–77**
- bats 78–79, **78–79**
- bird songs 90–91, **90–91**
- cat's eyes 66–67, **66–67**
- colorful 72–73, **72–73**
- dinosaur names 92–93, **92–93**
- eyelashes 24, **24**
- feeding zoo animals 52–53, **52–53**
- fireflies 80–81, **80–81**
- identification game 94–95, **94–95**
- monkeys 70–71, **70–71**
- penguins 84–85, **84–85**
- with pouches 74–75, **74–75**
- sniffing 64–65, **64–65**
- stinky animals 82–83, **82–83**
- ticklishness 20, **20**
- underground 68–69, **68–69**
- walrus tusks 86–87, **86–87**
- wolves 88–89, **88–89**
- yawning 23, **23**

Antarctica 84–85, **84–85,** 119, **119**
Antlers 76–77, **76–77**

B

Bacteria 18–19, 31, 125
Balls 48–49, **48–49,** 60–61, **60–61**
Baseball **51**
Basketball **50**
Bats 78–79, **78–79**
Beavers 87, **87**
Birds 73, **73,** 90–91, **90–91,** 125
Blood vessels 14–15
Blushing 14–15, **14–15**
Bolus 29
Brain 38, 39, 55
Bruises 15
Bubbles 40–41, **40–41,** 124
Burping 30–31, **30–31**
Burrowing owls 68, **68**
Butterflies 72–73, **72–73**

C

Caribou 77, **77**
Cats 17, **17,** 66
Cerebellum 38, 125
China 42, 59
Cold, body shivers 16–17, **16–17**
Colorful animals 72–73, **72–73**
Colors 120, **120,** 124
Corpse flower 111, **111**
Cotton candy 56–57, **56–57**
Crying 26–27, **26–27**

D

Dance 38–39, **38–39,** 124
Dandelions 112, **112**
Desert animals 68, **68**
Deserts 118–119, **118–119**
Dew 101, **101**
Digestive system **28–29,** 28–31, **30–31,** 125
Dinosaur names 92–93, **92–93,** 124
Dissolve, meaning of 57, **57,** 125
Dizziness 55, **55**
Dogs 10–11, **10–11,** 64, **64,** 124
Dolphins 99, **99**

E

Ear canals 55
Earth, rotation 120–121, **121**
Earthworms 69, **69**
Echolocation 78–79, **79**
Elephants 87, **87**
Embarrassment 14–15, **14–15**
Emperor penguins 84–85, **84–85**
Evaporation 102–103, **102–103,** 125
Exercise 12–13, **12–13,** 124
Eyebrows 25, **25**
Eyelashes 24, **24**
Eyes 26–27, **26–27,** 66–67, **66–67**

F

Feet 18–19, **18–19,** 84, **84**
Fireflies 80–81, **80–81,** 124
Fireworks 58–59, **58–59**
Fish, drinking water 99, **99**

Flowers 110–111, **110–111,** 125
Fog 100, **100**
Football **51**
Frogs 73, **73**
Fun and games 36–61
animal identification 94–95, **94–95**
bouncing balls 48–49, **48–49**
bubble shape 40–41, **40–41**
cotton candy 56–57, **56–57**
dizziness from spinning 55, **55**
fireworks 58–59, **58–59**
gardens 122–123, **122–123**
human body 34–35, **34–35**
kite tails **36–37,** 42–43, **42–43**
martial arts 46–47, **46–47**
music 38–39, **38–39**
pattern game 60–61, **60–61**
referee signals 50–51, **50–51**
roller coasters 54, **54**
swimming 44–45, **44–45**
zoo animals 52–53, **52–53**
Fungi 114–115, **114–115,** 125

G

Gardens
flowers 110–111, **110–111**
game 122–123, **122–123**
pumpkins 108–109, **108–109**
weeds 112–113, **112–113**
Gills 99, 125
Glowing animals 80–81, **80–81**
Goosebumps 17, **17**

H

Hair 25, 55
Happiness 39
Hearing, sense of 64
Heartbeat 12–13, **12–13,** 13, 38
Heat 104–105, **104–105**
Hockey **51**
Human body
see Me, myself, and I
Hunger 28, **28**

I

Ice hockey **51**

K

Kangaroos 74, **74,** 124
Kite tails **36–37,** 42–43, **42–43**
Koalas **75**

L

Larynx 9, 125
Lightning bugs 80–81, **80–81**

M

Mandarin duck **73**
Marsupials 74–75, **74–75**
Martial arts 46–47, **46–47**
Me, myself, and I 6–35
blushing 14–15, **14–15**
bruises 15
burping 30–31, **30–31**
crying 26–27, **26–27**
dizziness from spinning 55, **55**
eyebrows 25, **25**
eyelashes 24, **24**
game 34–35, **34–35**
goosebumps 17, **17**
heartbeat 12–13, **12–13**
mouth watering 29, **29**
music and dance 38–39, **38–39**
roller coasters 54, **54**
running 10–11, **10–11**
shadow 106, **106**
shivering 16–17, **16–17**
smell, sense of 65, **65**
sneezing 32–33, **32–33**
stinky feet 18–19, **18–19**
stomach growls 28, **28**
temperature 16
ticklishness 20–21, **20–21**
voice 8–9, **8–9**
yawning 22–23, **22–23**
Micropachycephalosaurus 93, **93**
Minmi 92, **92**
Monarch butterflies 72, **72–73**
Monkeys 20, 70–71, **70–71**
Moose 76, **76–77**
Mouth, watering 29, **29**
Movement 38–39, **38–39**
Mushrooms 114–115, **114–115**
Music 38–39, **38–39,** 124

N

Nature 96–123
deserts 118–119, **118–119**
dew 101, **101**
flowers 110–111, **110–111**
fog 100, **100**
gardens 122–123, **122–123**
mushrooms 114–115, **114–115**
ocean water 98–99, **98–99**
puddles 102–103, **102–103**
pumpkin seeds 108–109, **108–109**
shadows 106–107, **106–107**
sunrise and sunset 120–121, **120–121**
sunshine 104–105, **104–105**
trees 116–117, **116–117**
weeds 112–113, **112–113**
Nocturnal animals 68, 78–79, **78–79,** 125
Nostrils 64, 125

O

Ocean water 98–99, **98–99**
Opossums **75**
Owls 68, **68**

P

Pattern game 60–61, **60–61**
Penguins **62–63,** 84–85, **84–85**
Poison dart frogs 73, **73**
Pollination 110–111, **110–111**
Prairie dogs 69, **69**
Puddles 102–103, **102–103**
Pumpkin seeds 108–109, **108–109**

R

Rain puddles 102–103, **102–103**
Referees 50–51, **50–51**
Rhythm 39, 125
Roller coasters 54, **54**
Running 10–11, **10–11**

S

Sahara, Africa 118, **118**
Saliva 29
Salt water 98–99, **98–99**
Shadows 106–107, **106–107**
Shivering 16–17, **16–17**
Skin 14–15, **14–15,** 17, **17**
Skunks 82, **82**
Smell, sense of 64–65, **64–65**
Sneezing 32–33, **32–33**
Sniffing 64–65, **64–65**
Soccer **51**
Songbirds 90–91, **90–91,** 125
Speed 10–11, **10–11**
Spinning 55, **55**
Sports
bouncing balls 48–49, **48–49**
martial arts 46–47, **46–47**
referee signals 50–51, **50–51**
swimming 45–46, **45–46**
Squash 108–109, **108–109**
Stink bugs 83, **83**
Stinky animals 82–83, **82–83**
Stinky feet 18–19, **18–19**
Stomach 28, **28**
Sugar 56–57, **56–57**
Sunrise and sunset 120–121, **120–121**
Sunshine 104–105, **104–105**
Sweat 19
Swimming goggles 45, **45**
Swimming pools 44, **44**

T

Tears 26–27, **26–27**
Ticklishness 20–21, **20–21**
Trees 70–71, **70–71, 114–115,** 114–117, **116–117**
Try this!
bird songs 91, **91**
bouncy balls 49, **49**
dissolve sugar 57, **57**
Earth rotation 121, **121**
echolocation 79, **79**
evaporation 103, **103**
heartbeat test 13, **13**
shadows 107, **107**
sniffer test 65, **65**
tickle yourself 21, **21**
Tusks 86–87, **86–87,** 125

U

Underground animals 68–69, **68–69**

V

Vision, in cats 66–67
Voice 8–9, **8–9**
Vultures 83, **83**

W

Walruses 86–87, **86–87**
Warty comb jellyfish **81**
Water 98–99, **98–99,** 102–103, **102–103,** 125
Weeds 112–113, **112–113**
Wolves 88–89, **88–89**
Wombats **75**
Worms 69, **69**

Y

Yawning 22–23, **22–23,** 124

Z

Zoos 52–53, **52–53**

FOR BRIA & WILLIAM —J. E.

Since 1888, the National Geographic Society has funded more than 14,000 research, conservation, education, and storytelling projects around the world. National Geographic Partners distributes a portion of the funds it receives from your purchase to National Geographic Society to support programs including the conservation of animals and their habitats. To learn more, visit natgeo.com/info.

For more information, visit nationalgeographic.com, call 1-877-873-6846, or write to the following address:

National Geographic Partners, LLC
1145 17th Street NW
Washington, DC 20036-4688 U.S.A.

For librarians and teachers: nationalgeographic.com/books/librarians-and-educators

More for kids from National Geographic: natgeokids.com

For rights or permissions inquiries, please contact National Geographic Books Subsidiary Rights: bookrights@natgeo.com

Designed by Brett Challos

The publisher would like to acknowledge and thank early childhood learning specialist Barbara Bradley for her expert insights and guidance. Many thanks also to Megan Tucker and Monique Droussard and their families and to researcher Jennifer Geddes for their invaluable help with this book.

Library of Congress Cataloging-in-Publication Data
Names: Esbaum, Jill, author.
Title: Little kids first big book of why 2 / by Jill Esbaum.
Description: Washington, D.C. : National Geographic Kids, 2018. | Series: Little kids first big book | Includes index. | Audience: Pre-K.
Identifiers: LCCN 2017010963 (print) | LCCN 2017012748 (ebook) | ISBN 9781426330018 (e-book) | ISBN 9781426329999 (hardcover : alk. paper) | ISBN 9781426330001 (reinforced library binding : alk. paper)
Subjects: LCSH: Children's questions and answers.
Classification: LCC AG195 (ebook) | LCC AG195 .E83 2018 (print) | DDC 031.02--dc23
LC record available at https://lccn.loc.gov/2017010963

Printed in China
22/PPS/2

Photo Credits

AL = Alamy Stock Photo; DS = Dreamstime; GI = Getty Images; SS = Shutterstock

Cover: (flower), jurisam/iStockphoto; (feet), Alexandra Iakovleva/iStockphoto/GI; (penguin), J-L Klein & M-L Hubert; back cover: (fireworks), Kenneth Sponsler/iStockphoto; (cotton candy), Robert Clark/National Geographic Image Collection; spine, Iwona Grodzka/SS; 2 (UP LE), Jak Wonderly; 2 (RT), Andy Ryan/The Image Bank/GI; 2 (LO LE), LWA/Photographer's Choice/GI; 3 (UP), Henri Faure/DS; 3 (LO LE), Artville; 3 (LO CTR), topseller/SS; 3 (RT), Artville; 4-5, Hintau Aliaksei/SS; 6-7, Mint Images Limited/AL; 8, KidStock/Blend Images LLC/GI; 9, JGI/Jamie Grill/Blend Images/GI; 10-11, BJI/Blue Jean Images/GI; 11 (UP), Henri Faure/DS; 11 (LO), Kaliva/SS; 12, Image Source/Digital Vision/GI; 13 (RT), busayamol/SS; 13 (UP LE), aopsan/SS; 13 (LO LE), rangizzz/SS; 13 (LO inset), Fuse/Corbis RF Stills/GI; 14, JGI/Jamie Grill/Blend Images/GI; 15, Mac99/iStockphoto/GI; 16-17, Blend Images/Don Mason/Brand X/GI; 17 (UP), Upyanose/iStockphoto/GI; 17 (LO), Eric Isselée/SS; 18, Rosemarie Gearhart/iStockphoto/GI; 19 (UP), Tetra Image/AL; 19 (LO), Richard T. Nowitz/Corbis Documentary/GI; 20, Susan Kuklin/Science Source/GI; 21, Paul Bradbury/Caiaimage/GI; 22, picturepartners/SS; 23 (UP), Deshevykh_DN/iStockphoto; 23 (LO), Natalie Fobes/The Image Bank/GI; 24 (UP), David Troy/AL; 24 (LO), Jak Wonderly; 25, Andy Ryan/The Image Bank/GI; 26, sudo takeshi/Taxi/GI; 27 (UP), Jessie Jean/The Image Bank/GI; 27 (LO), Westend61/GI; 28-29, Alina Vincent/iStockphoto/GI; 30, Jacom Stephens/iStockphoto/GI; 31 (UP), Roberto Westbrook/Blend Images RM/GI; 31 (LO), DenisNata/SS; 32, antpkr/iStockphoto/GI; 33, Maxximmm/DS; 34, Mint Images Limited/AL; 35 (4), picturepartners/SS; 35 (6), Maxximmm/DS; 36-37, Bounce/Cultura RF/GI; 38 (LE), Xinhua/AL; 38 (RT), Daniel Dempster Photography/AL; 39, Hill Street Studios/Stockbyte/GI; 40, Patrick Foto/SS; 41 (LE), nikkytok/SS; 41 (RT), Blend Images-Jill Giardino/Brand X/GI; 42, Sven Gabriel/EyeEm/GI; 42-43, Henglein and Steets/Cultura RF/GI; 44, Mint Images/GI; 45, JaySi/SS; 46, Andrew Fox/Corbis Documentary/GI; 47 (martial arts belts), tzotzo/AL; 47 (LE), Scott Campbell/AL; 47 (RT), LWA/Photographer's Choice/GI; 48, Christopher Futcher/E+/GI; 49 (soccer ball), Daniel Thornberg/DS; 49 (basketball), Aaron Amat/SS; 49 (baseball), Dan Thornberg/SS; 49 (beach ball), Steshkin Yevgeniy/SS; 49 (tennis ball), Photodisc; 49 (RT), Mark Thiessen/NG Staff; 50, Rommel Canlas/SS; 51 (UP), A. T. Willett/AL; 51 (LO LE), Visions of America, LLC/AL; 51 (LO CTR), Visionhaus/Corbis via GI; 51 (LO RT), Andy Marlin/NHLI via GI; 52-53, Education Images/GI; 53, Purino/SS; 54, Jim West/AL; 55, Anastasia Tveretinova/SS; 56, Robert Clark/National Geographic Image Collection; 57 (glass of water), Andrey_Kuzmin/SS; 57 (spoon), Igor Kovalchuk/SS; 57 (sugar cubes), Givaga/SS; 57 (RT), Mark Burnett/Science Source; 58-59, Tuomaslehtinen/DS; 58, Taras Vyshnya/SS; 60-61 (football), Photodisc; 60-61 (basketball), Aaron Amat/SS; 60-61 (beach ball), Steshkin Yevgeniy/SS; 60-61 (soccer ball), Daniel Thornberg/DS; 62-63, Vladimir Seliverstov/DS; 64, Fly_dragonfly/SS; 65, Mark Thiessen/NG Staff; 66, Malcolm Schuyl/FLPA/Minden Pictures; 67 (UP), AfriPics.com/AL; 67 (LO), Scott Camazine/AL; 68, Tom Vezo/Minden Pictures; 69 (UP), Sean Kaufmann/Moment RF/GI; 69 (LO), D. Kucharski K. Kucharska/SS; 70-71, Thomas Marent/Minden Pictures; 72, Wilm Ihlenfeld/SS; 72-73, Cathy Keifer/SS; 73 (UP), Dirk Ercken/DS; 73 (LO), Wang LiQiang/SS; 74, Johncarnemolla/DS; 75 (UP), Rafael Ben-ari/DS; 75 (LO LE), Rob Jamieson/DS; 75 (LO RT), Cynthia Kidwell/SS; 76, Ron Erwin/All Canada Photos/GI; 77 (UP LE), Sergey Krasnoshchokov/SS; 77 (UP RT), Pi-Lens/SS; 77 (LO), Alfie Photography/SS; 78, Kheng Ho Toh/DS; 79 (UP LE), Mark Thiessen/NG Staff; 79 (LO LE), Mark Thiessen/NG Staff; 79 (RT), Mark Thiessen/NG Staff; 80-81, Floris van Breugel/NaturePL; 81 (UP), Solvin Zankl/AL; 81 (CTR), Jak Wonderly; 81 (LO), David Liittschwager/National Geographic Image Collection; 82, Ultrashock/SS; 83 (UP), Hway Kiong Lim/SS; 83 (LO), Carmine Arienzo/SS; 84 (UP), Paul Nicklen/National Geographic Image Collection; 84 (LO), Vladimir Seliverstov/DS; 85, Fred Olivier/Nature Picture Library; 86, Steven Kazlowski/Science Faction/GI; 87 (UP), Ron Sanford/Corbis Documentary/GI; 87 (LO), NightOwlZA/iStockphoto; 88-89, Edwin Giesbers/Nature Picture Library; 90, Paul Reeves/iStockphoto; 91, Cindy Prins/Moment RM/GI; 92-93, Franco Tempesta; 96-97, Georgette Douwma/Photographer's Choice/GI; 98, Tatiana Popova/SS; 99 (UP), Kletr/SS; 99 (LO), Willyam Bradberry/SS; 100, DenisTangneyJr/iStockphoto; 101 (UP), OJO Images Ltd/AL; 101 (LO), Hellen Grig/SS; 102, Roberto Westbrook/GI; 103 (empty plastic cups), Mark Thiessen/NG Staff; 103 (plastic wrap), Mark Thiessen/NG Staff; 103 (marker), TRINACRIA PHOTO/SS; 103 (rubber band), Feng Yu/SS; 103 (notebook), aopsan/SS; 103 (RT), Mark Thiessen/NG Staff; 104-105, Blend Images/AL; 104, mashab_7ya/iStockphoto; 106, Duncan McKenzie/Photographer's Choice/GI; 107 (UP), Mark Thiessen/NG Staff; 107 (LO), Mark Thiessen/NG Staff; 108, Blend Images/AL; 109 (UP LE), Artville; 109 (CTR LE), Cousin_Avi/SS; 109 (CTR RT), AN NGUYEN/SS; 109 (LO LE), Artville; 109 (LO RT), topseller/SS; 110, MMCez/SS; 110-111, Zeljko Radojko/SS; 111 (LO LE), Xinhua/AL; 111 (LO CTR LE), Rex May/AL; 111 (LO CTR RT), MYN/John Tiddy/Nature Picture Library; 111 (LO RT), Lori Epstein/National Geographic Image Collection; 112, karloss/SS; 112-113, Pinkcandy/SS; 114, WIN-Initiative/GI; 115 (UP LE), Nikolay Kurzenko/SS; 115 (UP RT), Jolanda Aalbers/SS; 115 (LO LE), JohnatAPW/SS; 115 (LO RT), Seaphotoart/SS; 116-117, Maximilian Müller/GI; 118, Valentin Armianu/DS; 119 (UP LE), Nataliya Hora/SS; 119 (UP RT), Stanislav Fosenbauer/SS; 119 (LO), Volodymyr Goinyk/iStockphoto; 120, Chilkoot/DS; 121 (UP LE), Petr Malyshev/SS; 121 (LO LE), Skypixel/DS; 121 (RT), Mark Thiessen/NG Staff; 122 (ear), Daizuoxin/DS; 122-123 (girl), Mark Thiessen/NG Staff; 122-123 (boy), theboone/iStockphoto; 123 (eyes), Naluwan/SS; 123 (flower), Jruffa/DS; 123 (butterfly), Sari ONeal/SS; 123 (bees on flower), MMCez/SS; 123 (hummingbird), Kts/DS; 125, Susan Schmitz/SS